# THE RELIGIOUS LIFE OF
# KING HENRY VI

HENRY VI

From the portrait in the National Portrait Gallery

# THE RELIGIOUS LIFE OF
# KING HENRY VI

BY     21473

## CARDINAL GASQUET

AUTHOR OF "HENRY VIII AND THE ENGLISH MONASTERIES,"
"THE EVE OF THE REFORMATION," ETC.

## LONDON
## G. BELL AND SONS, LTD.
### 1923

PRINTED IN GREAT BRITAIN.
CHISWICK PRESS : CHARLES WHITTINGHAM AND GRIGGS (PRINTERS), LTD.
TOOKS COURT, CHANCERY LANE, LONDON.

# FOREWORD

VERY few words are necessary to intro-
duce this small volume upon King
Henry VI. It deals mainly with his religious life and personal character, and not at
all with the political events of his reign or
with the sanguinary struggles between the
royal Houses of York and Lancaster for the
possession of the throne of England. Regarding the stirring episodes of the Civil
War of the Roses, and partly at least in consequence of the total collapse of Henry and
his murder in the Tower of London, our
modern historians in their account of this reign
have occupied themselves, not unnaturally,
but little with the personality of the unfortunate monarch. The entire destruction of
his royal authority has been considered as
sufficient to describe him briefly as a weak
and vacillating ruler, about whom little good
can be said: whilst the fact that for a brief
space of time his mental faculties gave way,

during which he was forced to live in seclusion, has probably been held to be more than sufficient to show that he was never, at any time, a prince worthy to reign over England.

Few people, who have taken their notions of this period of time from our modern school histories, will be disposed to think otherwise of this unfortunate monarch. There is, however, another side to this matter: that is, so far as his personal qualities are concerned, at one time, and for a long period of time, Henry VI was recognized and revered generally as one of the glories of the Kingdom. He was known in fact as the national saint of the country.

It was perhaps not unnatural that, after his death, the party that had dispossessed him of his throne and done him to death, should have endeavoured to prevent him from becoming a popular hero by lowering his character in the minds of the people generally. And so the notion that Henry was a weak-minded and useless ruler thus set forth was believed by a few contemporary authors, and found its way, for example, into the

writings of Pope Pius II. In England, however, from the first the murdered King was held
in veneration. He was regarded as a just and
upright ruler, and there sprang up all over
the country a popular devotion to him,
which the civil authorities could not suppress.
As it continued to grow, the process of the
canonization was begun in Rome at the instance of King Henry VII. The tomb of the
murdered King at Windsor became a place of
universal pilgrimage renowned for the multi-
tude of the miracles and favours granted by
God at his intercession.

During the religious changes of the sixteenth century these facts became obscured
and forgotten. It is the object of this book
to bring back to its readers what our ancestors
believed about holy King Henry VI.

*August* 1923.

# CONTENTS

# LIST OF ILLUSTRATIONS

# THE RELIGIOUS LIFE OF KING HENRY VI

## I

## HIS EARLY LIFE AND EDUCATION

KING HENRY VI was born at Windsor on 6th December 1421, the only son of Henry V and his wife, Catherine of France. He was baptized by Archbishop Chichely of Canterbury; his godparents being his uncle, John Duke of Bedford; his great-uncle, Henry Beaufort, Bishop of Winchester; and Jacqueline, Countess of Holland.

The premature death of his father, on 31st August 1422, made the infant King of England when only nine months old; Henry V's last directions in regard to his son were ignored, and Parliament appointed his eldest uncle, John Duke of Bedford, Protector of the little King. The real government of the kingdom, however, rested with the Council, and all writs were issued in the King's name. Henry V had appointed Sir Walter Hungerford to attend upon his son, but this disposition was set aside and the child remained for a time under his mother's care. As a baby he was brought from Windsor, and on 18th November 1423 was presented to the Parliament at Westminster. In the following January, Joan, the wife of Thomas Astley, was appointed his nurse by a writ issued in the King's name, and Dame Alice Butler was selected to attend his person with due licence " to chastise us reasonably from time to time." In 1425 the Council gave orders that the heirs of all baronies, etc., in the wardship of the Crown were to be brought up at the Court about the King's person, each one being provided with a master at the charge of the State. In this way the royal palace became " an academy for the young nobility."

In 1424 a letter was written in the name of the little King to Pope Martin V to petition for the canonization of St. Osmund of Salisbury, and this had the support of Archbishop Chichely of Canterbury.

Before Henry VI was four years old he was forced to take a personal part in public State functions. Thus in April 1425 he appeared at St. Paul's " led upon his feet, between the

Lord Protector and the Duke of Exeter, unto the choir, whence he was borne to the High Altar." After this ceremony he was "set upon a fair courser and so conveyed through Chepe and other streets of the city." * During the Parliament then in session Henry was "sundry times conveyed to Westminster, and within the Parliament Chamber kept his royal state."

In 1426 the small King opened the "Parliament of Bats" at which Bedford sought to end the dissensions between Gloucester and Bishop Beaufort. At this time, on Whit Sunday, the Protector dubbed his nephew a knight, and afterwards a number of young nobles received their knighthood from the "gracious hands" of the child King. The Christmas and the New Year of 1426 were kept by the Court at Eltham, and the little King received among his presents a set of coral beads which had belonged to King Edward, and was amused by the games and interludes of "Jack Travail" and his company, and by the music of "portable organs."†

* Fabyan's *Concordance of Histories,* quoted in the *D.N.B.*

† Rymer, *Foedera,* x, 387.

In the year 1428 Richard Beauchamp, Earl of Warwick, became the King's master. On 1st June the Earl was ordered " to be about the King's person " and directed " to teach him to love, worship, and dread God, draw him to virtue by ways and means convenable, laying before him examples of God's Grace to virtuous Kings, and the contrary fortunes of Kings of the contrary disposition, to teach him nurture, literature, languages and other manner of cunning, to chastise him when he doth amiss, and to remove persons not behovefull nor expedient from his presence." *

For his early training in religion and virtue the boy King had the advantage of the watchful care of Thomas Netter, or Walden, the learned and pious Carmelite, one of the most famous theologians of his day. Netter had been the Confessor of King Henry V, and in that capacity had accompanied him to France in 1422. The King was assisted in his last hours by the saintly Friar, and is said to have died in his arms. It was Netter who pronounced the funeral discourse over the body at its burial in Westminster Abbey on 6th November 1422.

* Rymer, *Foedera*, x, 399.

From that time the Carmelite was called upon to watch over the child King, and as Henry grew in intelligence he became his first spiritual guide and instructor and, in time, his first Confessor and Monitor. Netter went over to France in 1430 with the little King, but died at Rouen on 6th November of that year, being buried at the Carmelite Church in that city.

On 6th November 1429, when Henry was not yet nine years old, he was crowned at Westminster with due solemnity. The Earl of Warwick led him to the " high scaffold set up in the Abbey Church," where he sat " beholding the people all about sadly and wisely," and showing " humility and devotion." After this the Council declared the Protectorate at an end, and ordered that the young King should now visit his French dominions. So, after spending the Easter at Canterbury, conducted by Cardinal Beaufort he crossed over to Calais. His first act on landing at ten o'clock in the morning was to ride on horseback to attend High Mass at St. Nicholas' Church. On 16th December of this year, 1430, Henry was crowned King of France and returned to England in February

1431. On 12th May of the following year he opened Parliament in person, and was present at the fiery debates regarding the charges against Henry Beaufort, at the end of which he declared himself convinced of the loyalty of his great-uncle.

At this time the Earl of Warwick reported to the Council that the young King was now " grown in years, in ſtature of his person, and also conceit and knowledge of his royal Eſtate, the which cause him to grudge with chaſtising," and that " he hath been ſtirred by some from his learning, and spoken to of divers matters not behovefull." On this representation Warwick obtained fuller powers for the regulation of the royal household and the prohibition of all unauthorized persons to approach him. Henry himself was moreover admonished to obey the precepts of his maſter.

It is not necessary to follow the political hiſtory of this period in any detail. The Wars of the Roses and the changing fortunes of the King and his party during the civil diſturbances are sufficiently well known from our ordinary hiſtories. Our intereſt mainly, if not wholly, is to underſtand the religious dispositions of Henry VI and to see what, if any, evidence exists of an exceptional piety and religious sentiment on his part.

In 1433 the King, then a boy of twelve, went to the Abbey of Bury St. Edmund to pass the Christmas festivities. The Council, in fact, proposed to the Abbot that he should receive their royal master for a long period, and his visit to the monks lasted till St. George's Day 1434. The record of this visit states that to do honour to the guest the Abbot appointed a hundred officers of all ranks to attend upon him and his suite. Henry arrived on the eve of Christmas, and was solemnly received at the church door by Abbot Curteys and the community, and was conducted at once to pay his devotions at the shrine of the Martyr King behind the High Altar.

The King took part in all the religious ceremonies of the time, joining in the festivities and making himself acquainted with every part of the vast establishment. After the Epiphany he dispensed with the more ceremonious observances of the Abbot's palace and, taking up his abode with the Prior, enjoyed with his courtiers a mild kind of hunting. Later he went to the Abbot's house at Elmswell and divided his time between fishing and hawking until the vigil of the Purification, when he returned to Bury to be present at the blessing of the Candles. The season of Lent was again passed in the Prior's lodgings, and the youthful King was present at all the solemn ceremonies of the Holy Week and Easter.

On the Tuesday after the feast, Henry, together with the Earl and Countess of Warwick, was formally received into the fraternity of the Convent of Bury. Humphrey, Duke of Gloucester, who was with the King and who was already a Confrater of St. Alban's Monastery, petitioned to become a member of the family of St. Edmund's also. The young monarch determined that the reception should be carried out in the most formal manner possible, so, having prostrated himself before the shrine of St. Edmund, followed by the Duke of Gloucester, the Earl of Warwick, and the rest of his suite, he proceeded to the Chapter House where the monks were assembled, and there asked for the privilege of being joined in brotherhood with the monks. Then the Duke of Gloucester on his knees begged the King to thank the Abbot and the brethren of Edmundsbury for all their kindness to him during his stay; and the King, taking Abbot Curteys by the hand, "gleefully and gladly thanked him again and again," and affectionately commended himself to God, St. Edmund, and to the prayers of the Abbot and his brethren. So intimate did the King become with the monks on this visit that during the rest of his life he constantly returned to Edmundsbury to renew his acquaintance with the monks and to demand the protection and assistance of St. Edmund, the Martyr King. A long account of this visit is printed in Dugdale's *Monasticon*, in which there is a miniature of the young King praying before the shrine of St. Edmund. This picture is taken from the life of the saint written at the time by the monk-poet Lydgate, and presented to the monarch at the time of his visit.

In 1442 Henry reached his legal majority, and three years later married Margaret of Anjou. In the summer of the following year, 1446, the King and his court made a tour of the monasteries in England and paid his devotions at the celebrated shrine of Our Lady of Walsingham. In this same year Pope Eugenius IV sent him the "Golden Rose," and the Brief, dispatched with it from Rome, describes the blessing given to this gift on the previous *Laetare* Sunday. Both going to and returning from the church, in which the Pope celebrated Mass on that day, the Holy Father carried the golden ornament in his hand so that it might be seen by all the people through whose ranks he passed, and in his letter the Holy Father says that he is sending the " Rose " to Henry " having regard to his great faith and devotion to Him and the Holy Roman Church, which make it not only proper but rightly due to him " to receive this present.

In 1459 King Henry came to keep the feast of Easter at St. Albans. Abbot Whethamstede in his chronicle, describing the visit, says: " At the time when Our Lord came to Jerusalem, sitting on an ass to keep the Pasch with His disciples, the Lord King came also to the Monastery with his nobles, barons, knights and his suite to eat the Paschal Lamb." When the Easter celebrations were over Henry proposed to return at once to London, but before setting out, he bade the guardian of the royal wardrobe give to the Prior his best state robe, which he had worn only on Easterday, and

HENRY VI AT THE SHRINE OF ST. EDMUND

From Lydgate's Life of St. Edmund (MS. Harl. 2278)

which he intended to present to St. Alban's Shrine. His treasurer, however, later promised to give the monastery fifty marks in place of this royal robe of state, and on the day of the King's departure the Prior, acting for the Abbot who was ill, came to thank the King for all the benefits he had already bestowed upon the Abbey, and to beg for a continuation of the royal favour. To this speech the King replied: " Father Prior, we have so far done little for you, but if by the grace of God's mercy we are allowed to live a little longer we will abundantly increase our benefactions to you, so that you may have reason and material cause to pray in a special manner for us." The King after leaving his apartments went to pray again at the shrine, and thence passing out of the great west door of the church, mounted his horse. Before starting, he turned to the Prior and reminded him that he was to come as soon as possible to London to receive the sum of money promised to the convent in place of the state robe he had given to St. Alban's Shrine. This the Prior did forthwith; and on his arrival at the royal palace Henry received him at once and directed that the money should be brought, and he himself

counted it out and handed it over to the Prior.
At the same time he bade the keeper of the
royal wardrobe provide a piece of the most
precious cloth of gold " commonly called
crimson tissue," sufficiently large to make a
cope, chasuble, and two tunicles for use at the
High Altar of the great Martyr. At the close
of the interview the King addressed the Prior
thus: " Father Prior, these things are a small,
and indeed very small or rather no return at all
for the spiritual favours, which are worth
greatly more, but as we intend later to bestow
other gifts, we desire your Abbot and Convent
to grant us one favour more: that is, to keep
after our decease the anniversary of our death,
and by a written document to assure us of this
favour."

On his return to St. Albans the Prior
informed the Abbot of this request, and in
Chapter the convent forthwith drew up and
sealed a letter of Fraternity for the King and
promised to observe for ever his annual obit.

It is worthy of remark that throughout his
life Henry was delighted, whenever he could,
to pass some time in the seclusion of some
religious house. John Ross, the Warwickshire chronicler, and a contemporary of the

saintly monarch, relates that he " well remembered, whilst he was in the schools at Oxford, that King Henry VI, whenever he was in those parts was wont to make some stay with the [Carmelite] Friars there, just as if he was in his own palace." * Indeed, in the midst of all the troubles of his reign: in the varying changes of his fortune: in his successes and defeats during the Wars of the Roses, Henry sought for consolation in religion and in the society of religious men. He spent the Christmas of 1459-60 with the Canons of Leicester, and in the Lent of 1460 he passed three days in prayer before the shrine of St. Guthlac at Crowland. On Palm Sunday, the 29th of March 1461, Edward IV, then in possession of the throne, gained a decisive battle at Towton. Henry was not present in the field since, as is said, he " preferred to pass so holy a day in prayer at York." At one time during Henry's wanderings in the north to escape from his enemies, he took refuge in a monastery and lived there for a time disguised in the habit of a monk.

On the 4th of May 1471 the decisive battle of Tewkesbury was fought, when Queen

* *Chron. J. Rossi*, ed. Hearne, p. 192.

Margaret was defeated and Henry saw his only son Edward slain. Once again Henry was lodged in the Tower of London, having been long a prisoner in the hands of his enemies. On the 21st of the same month of May the deposed King was murdered, as all the world believed, by Richard Duke of Gloucester, brother of King Edward IV. The most circumstantial account says that Henry died " on Tuesday night 21 May, betwixt XI and XII of the clock, the Duke of Gloucester being then at the Tower and many others."

Speed, the historian, gives the following account of the murder and burial of the saintly King. " The bodey of this murthered King was upon Ascension-eve laid in an open coffin, and from the Tower, guarded with many bils and glaves, was carried through the streetes unto the Cathedrall Church of Saint Paul, where it rested uncovered one day, and began to bleed again afresh, a sorrowful spectacle to most of the beholders, and thence was it carryed to the Black Fryers Church, where it likewise lay barefaced, and bled as before, all men being amazed at the sorrowfull sighte; and lastly, it was put into a Boat, without priest, cloake, torch or taper, singing or saying, and was ferried into the Abbey of Chertsey in Surrey, and there without pompe interred." *

Shakespeare represents the universal opinion of the time regarding Henry's murder.

> *Gloucester.* Clarence, excuse me to the King my
>   brother
> I'll hence to London, on a serious matter
> Ere ye come there, be sure to hear some news.
>   *Clarence.* What ? What ?
>   *Gloucester.*              The Tower, the Tower !

then in the prison:

> *Enter Gloucester.*
>
> *Gloucester.* Good day, my lord ! What at your book so
>   hard ?

Then when Gloucester had dismissed the lieutenant King Henry says:

> So flies the reckless shepherd from the wolf :
> So first the harmless sheep doth yield his fleece,
> And next his throat unto the butcher's knife.
> What scene of death hath Roscius now to act ?

Then, after some words, Henry asks:

> But wherefore dost thou come ? Is 't for my life ?
>   *Gloucester.* Think'st thou, I am an executioner ?

* Speed, *The Historie of Great Britaine.*

*K. Henry.* A persecutor, I am sure thou art.
If murdering innocents be executing,
Why, then thou art an executioner.

\*         \*         \*         \*

*Gloucester.* I'll hear no more. Die, prophet, in thy
        speech ;
For this, amongst the rest, was I ordained. [*Stabs him.*
*K. Henry.* Ay, and for much more slaughter after this.
O God ! forgive my sins and pardon thee.

Then, in the play of *King Richard III*,* Shakespeare again represents Gloucester as the murderer of King Henry. Anne, the wife of the slain Prince Edward, is shown as following the bier of the King whilst it is being borne towards Chertsey, where the corpse was buried after having been exposed at St. Paul's and also for a time at Black Friars, where it is said to have bled, in the sight of the people. The most reliable account says that it was carried to Chertsey in a barge on the Thames, but the poet represents it as being taken by road.

*Anne.* Set down, set down your honourable load,
If honour be shrouded in a hearse.
Whilst I awhile obsequiously lament
The untimely fall of virtuous Lancaster,
Poor key-cold figure of a holy King !
Pale ashes of the house of Lancaster !
Thou bloodless remnant of that royal blood !

* Act I, scene ii.

Then when Gloucester comes on the scene
Anne points to the corpse, exclaiming:

If thou delight to view thy heinous deeds
Behold the pattern of thy butcheries!
O, Gentlemen, see, see! dead Henry's wounds
Open their congeal'd mouths, and bleed afresh!
Blush, blush, thou lump of foul deformity;
For 'tis thy presence that exhales this blood
From cold and empty veins, where no blood dwells.

*　　　*　　　*　　　*

Thou was provoked by thy bloody mind,
That never dreamt on aught but butcheries.
Didst thou not kill this King?

*Gloucester.*　　　　　　　　I grant thee.

*Anne.* Dost grant me, hedgehog? then God grant
me too
Thou may'st be damned for that wicked deed!
O! he was gentle, mild and virtuous.

*Gloucester.* The fitter for the King of heaven, that
hath him.

*Anne.* He is in heaven, where thou shalt never come.

*Gloucester.* Let him thank me, that holp to send him
thither,

For he was fitter for that place than earth.

## II

# KING HENRY'S RELIGIOUS LIFE

IN passing to the consideration of the inner life of Henry VI, at the outset it may be useful to state that, in spite of the many political enemies of the King, there has never, from the first, been any breath of scandal or reproach against his reputation. That he was a weak and vacillating ruler is about all that has ever been said against him. His weakness he inherited probably from his Lancastrian ancestors, and his impaired mind, which he manifested for a brief period at one time of his reign, came almost certainly from his connection with the family of Charles VI of France. Fortunately for our present purpose there has been preserved an intimate account of the King's private life, written by his chaplain and private secretary, one John Blackman, who, after the death of his royal master, entered the Carthusian Order. The author solemnly declares that in this life he has set down only what was within his own personal knowledge, or what he had learnt from absolutely trustworthy sources and unimpeachable witnesses. There is some reason to believe that the life was composed in the reign of Henry VII to be presented to the Pope as part of the evidence required for the proposed canonization of the saintly King.

Blackman thus prefaces his interesting account of the holy King: " Like another Job he was a man *simplex et rectus*, fearing the Lord God in all things and shunning evil. He was truly a *vir simplex* without any trace of deceit or double-dealing, as is admitted by everyone. He never treated anyone in a double manner, nor was he false to his people, but ever spoke with frankness. He was *rectus et justus* and always acted on the principles of justice. He never did anyone an injustice knowingly, nor did he ever do an injury to anyone. Most faithfully he rendered unto God what was His. He most carefully and amply gave to God and His Church the tithes and oblations due to them. In regard to religious worship, even when wearing his robes of state with the crown on his head, he was wont to show to God profound reverence; to make his bows and inclinations and to say his prayers, as if he were some young religious."

The Prince manifested a filial fear of God by numberless acts of devotion. One of the English bishops of his time used to say that, having been his Confessor for ten years, he could declare that during all that time no stain of grievous sin had ever tarnished his soul. " Oh! What constant care: oh! what diligent watchfulness to please God was found in this exalted young person. *Attendite reges et principes universi, juvenes et virgines et populi quique, et laudate Dominum in Sanctis ejus.* Imitate the virtue of this King, who could have done evil and did it not, but during his whole life, he shunned evil as far as he was able, because of God's displeasure."

King Henry was a constant and true worshipper of God. Indeed, he was more devoted to God's service and to the practice of devout prayer than to any worldly business or mundane matters, or to the playing of games or suchlike occupations. Mere frivolous things were abhorrent to him, and he assiduously practised himself in prayer, in the reading of the Holy Scriptures, or the study of history. From these he drew many useful lessons for his own spiritual consolation and for that of others. For this reason he was constantly consulted by, and gave helpful advice to, many in every state and condition of life and of every age; the young he exhorted to fly from vice and cultivate virtue. Many of older age than he and, indeed, even priests he urged to strive to grow in virtue and thus to make sure of the reward of eternal life. He was wont to quote to them the words of the Psalmist: "*Ite de virtute in virtutem. Videbitur enim tunc Deus Deorum in Syon.*"

King Henry's devout attitude in church was most noteworthy. He never liked to make use of a seat, or to move about, as is the custom of worldly-minded people. His head was always uncovered during the celebration of the divine offices: he rarely raised his eyes but almost always remained on his knees before a book, following, with his eyes on his missal and with his hands partly raised, the epistles and gospels said by the celebrant. To the wonder of many people he used to send letters full of holy and salutary advice to some of his clerics.

Wherever the King might be, he manifested a special devotion to the Holy Cross.

He was ever faithful in his worship, in his reception of the Sacraments, and in all the holy practices of the Christian religion. Whilst at his devotions, he was wont to sit in a reverent attitude with his head uncovered. Even on a journey when riding on horseback, whilst making his wonted reverence to some wayside cross, he would often have fallen to the ground but for his attendants. He preferred to have crosses on his royal crown rather than leaves and flowers. He was accustomed to be at the Divine service early, and always before the beginning; and he never wearied at the length of the offices, even when they were protracted after midday. He would never allow swords to be worn in church, nor did he permit talking or the discussion of any business in the sacred places, but he strictly bade all his nobles and attendants to devote the time of prayer to prayer, in accordance with the word of our Lord: *Domus mea domus orationis est.* This he did himself with great and manifest devotion.

From his earliest childhood King Henry showed himself modest and pure. As a youth he carefully abstained from any word or act contrary to the virtue of chastity, and he lived his married life as a chaste, Christian husband. As an example of the purity of his life it may be mentioned that he avoided all immodesty of dress and, having the example of King David before his mind, he made a covenant with his eyes never to look at any woman with sinful pleasure. On one occasion whilst the young people at the Court were enjoying some Christmas dances, one of the great lords of the Court brought into the hall some female performers who were very scantily dressed and presented them to the young King. This, says Blackman, the author of this life, was " perhaps to test his virtue or to ensnare his young soul." Henry, however, " not taken off his habitual guard and recognizing the snare of the devil, was highly indignant. He lowered his eyes, and quickly turning his back, left the apartment saying: ' Fye, fye for shame, foresooth ye be to blame.' "

At another time, whilst riding through the city of Bath, where are the hot springs, in which the people of those parts are accustomed to bathe, the King, looking into the bath, saw men with all their clothes off and practically naked. He at once left the place, regarding such nudity as a crime, not forgetting the saying of Francesco Petrarch: *Nuditas beluina in hominibus non placet, sed pudore amiĉtus honeſtate consulitur*. Moreover, the monarch took the greateſt care not only to safeguard his own chaſtity, but carefully watched over his household in such matters. He was determined that no loose woman should ever enter his palace to effeĉt the ruin of any of his servants, if he could help it. He provided upright and virtuous prieſts to watch over his half-brothers, Jasper and Edmund, to teach them learning and virtue. Indeed, he always had the same care for all who were in attendance upon him, conſtantly warning them to avoid vicious and dissolute company and to pursue a life of virtue.

The saintly young King showed himself always anxious to avoid the peſt of avarice, by which many worldly princes are infeĉted, and in consequence of which so many fall. His mind was never captivated by any unlawful love for the magnificent presents he received, nor by the great riches which at one time he possessed. To the poor he was ever moſt liberal and always ready to help them in their needs. Indeed, he enriched very many by his gifts and by the offices he conferred upon them, and in this way raised many from want to fortune. He certainly never oppressed his people by any immoderate demands, as other princes and rulers before him had done. He lived indeed as a loving father among his children, relieving his peoples' wants out of his own revenues, and preferring to live upon his own resources rather than see his people oppressed by any hard exactions. He was ever entirely contented with what he had, and never coveted what others possessed. This can be shown by many examples. Once a great lord gave him a very precious canopy for his bed. It was covered with golden embroidery, and the donor, when making the presentation, said: *De talibus sit cura veſtra.* But the King, having his mind turned rather to the things heavenly and spiritual, showed clearly that he thought little of such gifts.

At another time the executor of the will of Cardinal Beaufort, Bishop of Wincheſter and uncle of His Majeſty, came to give him the great sum of £1,000 in gold for his own use and to lighten the burden of the State. Henry absolutely refused to touch the money, saying that he was grateful to his uncle, but added: " Do what you like with it, we have no desire

to have it." Much aſtonished at this attitude
of the King, the executors begged him at leaſt
to receive the gift towards the endowment of
the two colleges, which he had lately founded
at Cambridge and Eton. This he consented
to do, ordering them to pass on the gift to
these eſtablishments, for prayers for the soul
of the Cardinal.

Rare piety, loving charity, and an entire
resignation were found united in this saintly
prince. When at length he was despoiled of
his kingdoms of France and England, which
previously he had ruled, and was ſtripped of
all his goods and possessions, he bore his ill
fortune with a perfeſtly calm mind, regarding
all temporal goods as nought, so long as he
could possess Chriſt and the things of eternity.

Though he was open-handed in giving
temporal assiſtance, Henry was cautious and
prudent in conferring spiritual benefices. He
feared that he might perhaps be giving them
to men who were unworthy, or who had
obtained them in an improper manner, that is
to say, by simony. This care is evidenced by
the upright ecclesiaſtics he aſtually advanced
to office, and no suspicion of simony could at
any time be alleged againſt him. He was

ever intent on finding men of virtue and advancing them. He was truly inflamed with the fire of God's charity. When he appointed William Waynfleet to succeed the celebrated Cardinal Beaufort in the see of Winchester he said, in appointing him: " Receive your enthronization to Winchester and be there what former bishops have been. May you be long lived in this world, ever walking and going forward in the paths of virtue." With like intentions he promoted the Bishops of Worcester and Chester and others, as is known to all.

During his reign the King set up and endowed with ample estates and revenues two renowned colleges to the honour of God and to embellish the divine worship. In these colleges, which were intended for the support of many poor scholars, the divine offices were to be celebrated daily in praise of God Almighty. The students were to be exercised continuously in scholastic *dogmata* and other methods proper to foster the increase of learning.

In beginning his two colleges, he sought everywhere to secure the best " living stores "; that is, young men well grounded in virtue and learned priests who were already known as scholars and teachers. For this reason he said to the agent he was employing on this matter: "We would rather tolerate those who were weak in music than in their knowledge of the scripture." In regard to the boys and youths who were proposed to him as scholars, the first thing required by the King was that they should be trained in virtue, as well as in book learning. And so, from time to time, when he would meet, at the castle of Windsor, any of these youths who had come to see some of the royal household whom they knew, Henry, on recognizing that they were his boys, would urge them to follow along the path of virtue, and, giving them money, would say: "Be good boys, mild, docile, and servants of the Lord." If he found any of these youths visiting servants of his house, he would punish them and forbid them to do such a thing again. He feared that his lambs might learn bad practices and morals from his servants, or at least lose their own good practices in part or altogether from the contact, like the lambs and sheep which are pastured among thorns and briars and which tear their wool and often leave it entirely torn off.

Speaking of King Henry's humility, the writer Blackman says that it must first be understood that he was specially devoted to this virtue. He was never ashamed to act as the server of any priest celebrating Mass in his presence, answering: *Amen. Sed libera nos a malo*, etc. This, says Blackman, he often did " to me an unworthy priest."

At table, even at a short repast, Henry always finished " as religious do," by rising quickly, standing for a moment in silence, and every time devoutly rendering thanks to God. Master Doctor Town testifies that the King ordered his almoner always to place in front of him on the table at every meal a plaque, having upon it a representation of the Five Wounds of Christ as if wet with His blood. Before any course was served he would devoutly gaze upon the image, and renew his devotion to God.

It is related of him that riding one day along a road, he stopped to rest outside a cemetery at the east side of the church. At the time the Blessed Sacrament was not in the pyx hanging over the altar and, to the astonishment of his suite, Henry did not remove his hat, as he was always accustomed to do out of

his great devotion and reverence for the
Sacrament. In explaining to his lords why, in
this instance, he had not shown his usual
reverence to the place, he said: "I know that
my Lord Jesus Christ, in whose honour I
would do so much, is not there." It was afterwards found that this was the case, and that
the Blessed Sacrament was not, at the time,
in the pyx over the altar. It is also said by
those who were in the King's confidence, that
he frequently had a vision of our Lord in
human form in the priest's hands during the
Sacrifice of the Holy Mass. On the eve of
our Lord's resurrection the King was wont
himself to carry the great Paschal candle, out
of reverence, and to manifest his faith in the
resurrection of Christ from the tomb.

King Henry's humility was made apparent
to all in his clothes and the other coverings of
his body; in his walk, in his speaking, and in
his countenance. From his youth he was
accustomed to make use of rounded shoes and
leggings, such as country folk use. He
generally wore a long cloak with a round hood,
like those of the middle classes, with a tunic
coming down below the knee; his short
leggings and shoes were of dark colour, and

he was accustomed to forbid any novel fashion of dress for himself.

On the chief feasts of the year and in particular on the annual celebration of his coronation, he always wore a hair-shirt next to his skin, so that by the sharp pain of the cloth he might remember to shun all thoughts of luxury, and that every idea of pride or vainglory, which are too prone to arise under such circumstances, might be instantly repressed.

Many people still living, writes Blackman in the reign of King Henry VII, can speak of the way in which the King occupied his time during life. Sundays and other solemn festivals he always spent in hearing the divine offices and in devout prayer, both for himself and his people. Lest his enemies should have cause to laugh at his Sunday practices, he earnestly tried to induce others to follow his example; and for this reason some who at times attended upon him assert that his greatest pleasure and delight was in following exactly and with devotion the services of the Church. The less solemn days he did not spend in mere idleness or useless vanities: " *non in commessationibus aut ebrietatibus, non in vaniloquiis aut coeteris nocivis dictis aut loquelis*" (which, indeed, during all his life he avoided, using always few words, except such as were edifying and useful to others). But on these days he spent much time in treating of the necessary business of the country with his Council, or in reading no less diligently the Scriptures, or such serious writings like the Chronicles of various countries. As to this matter an honourable knight, once his devoted Chamberlain, named Richard Tunstall, has testified both by word and in writing that " *in lege Domini fuit voluntas ejus die ac nocte.*" In proof of this he declared that " the Lord King complained to me once in his room at Eltham, when I was alone with him and working with him over his holy books, and hearing his serious admonitions and his devout ejaculations, one of the most powerful of the English dukes knocked at the door. The King said: See how they disturb me!' I can hardly find time in the day or the night to refresh myself by the reading of sacred teachings because of these disturbances." The same thing, says the Chaplain Blackman, happened to me once at Windsor Castle.

In proof of King Henry's devotion to God, Blackman declares that there are many still

D

alive who were on terms of intimacy with him, who assert that he was wont continually to raise his eyes to heaven like one in a heavenly ecstasy, and that at times he seemed quite unconscious of himself or of those round about him. He was as a man out of himself, as one, whilst still on earth, having his conversation in heaven, according to the words of the Apostle: " *Conversatio nostra in coelis est.*"

Henry was never known to make use of any oath in order to enforce his orders. His only expression was the expression " Forsoothe and forsoothe." Indeed, he broke many of the lords and others of the habit of swearing, by his mild advice and even by harsh correction. Anyone swearing was regarded most unfavourably by him. On one occasion, hearing one of the great lords, who was his Chamberlain, suddenly utter an oath, he gave him a severe admonition, saying: " Alas! You the Lord of a great family and household, when you swear in this manner against the commandment of God, set a bad example to your servants and those subject to you. You provoke them, indeed, to do the same."

There are many examples of the patience and loving kindness which this King exercised

throughout his life. To give one instance
only: Once on a time, when coming from his
villa at St. Albans and passing through
Cripplegate into London, he saw over the
gateway the quarters of a traitor, who had
been proved to have been false to His
Majesty. Henry at once said: " Remove
this, I do not wish that any Christian should
be treated so cruelly for my sake." One who
was present has given testimony of this fact.

Again, when four noble gentlemen were
convicted of high treason and sentenced by
the judges to a felon's death, the King
remitted the penalty, sending at once to the
place of execution their pardon and an order
for their release. Three other great barons of
the realm conspired against the King and
gathered together a great number of armed
men to further the ambition of one of them
who, as after events showed, aspired to the
throne. Henry showed them great mercy and
pardoned them all—the leaders as well as their
followers, on condition that they submitted to
him.

There are many other instances of King
Henry's merciful disposition. In one case,
two men having conspired to kill him, one

actually inflicted a serious wound on his neck in an attempt to cut off his head. The King took this most patiently, only saying: " Forsoothe and forsoothe, ye do most foully to smyte a King anointed so." Indeed, Henry bore with absolute patience all the ill-treatment, the malignity, and the blasphemies of his enemies, after he was made a prisoner in the Tower.

" I do not think it right to pass over in silence," writes Blackman, " the heavenly favours bestowed upon this King." At the Easter time when he was a prisoner in the Tower of London, one of his chaplains expressed to him astonishment at the way he could possess his soul in peace at that holy time in spite of all his troubles. The King replied by saying: " I do so by recalling the heavenly kingdom to which I have looked forward from my infancy, and I do not care much for this transitory and earthly kingdom. I only want one thing, and that is that I may receive the Sacrament of this Paschal time with other Christians, on the *die Coenae* (Maunday Thursday) as is our custom." He often was granted, as has been said, a vision of our Lord in the hands of the priest celebrating

Mass in his presence. One of his secretaries living at Waltham testifies to revelations made to the King for three years in succession on St. Edward's Day. Also that on the Epiphany the Glory of the Lord was manifested to him in bodily form, crowned; and that on the Assumption the body and soul of the Blessed Virgin was shown to him being transported into heaven.

He is said, too, to have multiplied bread to feed his soldiers when they were in need, and many other favours granted by God in answer to his prayers are recorded by Blackman in his life of the saintly King. When a fugitive from his enemies it was revealed to him that he would be betrayed and taken prisoner to London. These revelations were made to him by our Blessed Lady, Saint John the Baptist, St. Dunstan, and St. Anselm, and they consoled him and helped him to bear his sufferings with an exemplary patience and fortitude. The saintly King's love for holy Scripture is attested by his possession of a magnificent copy of the Bible in English, which he presented to the monks of the London Charter House.

# III

## KING HENRY'S FOUNDATIONS AT ETON AND CAMBRIDGE

SOMETHING has already been said about the two colleges the King founded at Eton and Cambridge. It will perhaps be interesting to add some more details about these foundations, especially as the fact of the King having thus worked for sound Christian education was one of the matters urged upon the Popes in the petitions of King Henry VII to secure his canonization. These colleges still remain, lasting monuments of the love of their pious founder for learning and religion.

Besides these two great establishments the pious King had already taken a personal interest in the University of Caen, established in his name when he was a child by the Duke of Bedford. He had, moreover, encouraged others by every means in his power to assist learning and piety by making other similar foundations. The college at Eton was professedly an imitation of that of Winchester, and whole passages of its original statute were taken from those drawn up by the great Bishop William of Wykeham for his college. Each of these two schools were intended to be connected with a college at one or other of the Universities. Winchester was the natural approach to New College at Oxford, established by Bishop William of Wykeham, and Eton was designed in the same way to feed King's College, Cambridge, also founded by King Henry.

The intention of the royal founder was not merely to have a school for secular learning. He had the further design to make Eton a nursery of piety and sound religion. He first converted the parish church of the place into a collegiate establishment and richly endowed it. In this College of priests he ordained that there should be celebrated the perpetual worship of Almighty God in the Divine offices, and directed that daily intercession be made for his soul, as its founder. Joined to this collegiate body he placed a school, in which seventy scholars were to be taught for the priesthood, free of all cost. He hoped that this school would attract also many of the

ETON COLLEGE CHAPEL, LUPTON'S TOWER, AND SCHOOL YARD

From an etching by F. Buckler (c. 1814)

sons of the great English families and of the lesser gentry of the country to share in the Christian education provided for his scholars.

It is easy to understand the King's intention from the document still preserved, known from its opening words as " the Kynge's own devyse." This is a statement of his original intentions for his colleges of Eton and Cambridge. At the former the church was planned on the most magnificent scale and was to be ornamented in the most lavish manner. Besides the High Altar there were to be at least four others. There were also to be images of the Holy Trinity, of St. Anne, St. Andrew, St. Clement, etc., and a large representation of the Assumption of Our Blessed Lady known as " Our Lady of Eton "; and this became in time the object of great popular veneration.

There can be no sort of doubt that the primary object of the pious founder was to secure the service of God in the church. For the maintenance of this with fitting decorum he founded his college of priests, consisting of a Provost, ten Fellows, and ten Chaplains. Besides these he instituted ten clerks skilled in Church music and sixteen choristers under twelve years of age to sing and serve in the daily services.

From the first there were seven masses celebrated daily with due solemnity. The first was the Mass of Our Lady, to be offered to God for the soul of the founder and for the needs of the Church; the second was said for all benefactors, and the third was the High Mass of the day. The other masses were said for varying intentions at some of the side altars.

Great Indulgences were obtained by the pious King for his royal foundation from Pope Eugenius IV, and special privileges were granted on the occasion of a great pilgrimage to take place annually on the feast of Our Lady's Assumption. It was proposed in the first instance that the Indulgences to be gained by the faithful should be the same as those that could be obtained by visiting the Church of S. Pietro ad Vincula in Rome; but within a year this was changed by the Pope into a Plenary Indulgence to be gained by all on the usual conditions. We find it recorded, that in this way a great number of pilgrims were attracted year by year to the shrine of Our Lady of Eton on the feast of the Assumption,

15th August, and that the confessions of the people who desired to obtain the Indulgences were so numerous at times that the resident clergy, being unable to deal with the concourse, additional clerical assistance had to be secured. At one time, in 1444-5, the account roll shows that a sum of money was paid for the hire of thirty beds for these extra confessors and their servants.

It has already been pointed out that to this great collegiate establishment King Henry added a school to provide education for seventy poor scholars, who were to receive their teaching and maintenance free of all cost. It was also the royal intention that other boys should be admitted who might be attracted thither in order to share in the excellent educational advantages at Eton and who would pay for themselves. These latter " commensales," as they were called, were to live in the town with persons licensed to receive them. The life of the boys at school was severe. Early rising was enforced. On Sundays and Holy days, for instance, they rose at four o'clock. On such days no study work was done; but they had to attend all the divine offices and High Mass. On other days, as they had not to be present at Mattins, they rose an hour later and recited amongst themselves the Office of Our Lady. At six o'clock they had their morning prayers and the study work of the day began. There was an interruption between nine and ten to allow the boys to go across to the church and be present at the Elevation of the High Mass. They knelt down at the entrance, adored the Blessed Sacrament, and having said the verse *Adoremus Te Christe*, went back to their studies. During the dinner one of the scholars read aloud the Holy Scripture, the lives of the saints, or passages chosen from some doctor of the Church.

Speaking of the two colleges of Eton and Cambridge, the historian Stowe writes: "This year [1443] King Henry being of himself alwaies naturally inclined to do good, and fearing least he might seem unthankful to Almighty God for the great benefits bestowed upon him since the time he first took upon him the regiment of his realme, determined for his primer notable worke, to erect and found two famous colleges in honour and worship of His holy name, and for the increase of virtue, the dilation of cunning and establishment of

Christian Faith; whereof the one at Cambridge to be called his college Royall of Our Ladye and St. Nicholas; and the other at Eton, beside Windsore, to be called his college of our Blessed Ladie."

The official correspondence of Thomas Beckynton, secretary of King Henry VI, and subsequently Bishop of Bath and Wells,* proves the anxiety of the King to make his foundation at Eton permanent. This Bishop Beckynton was consecrated to the see of Bath and Wells on 13th October 1443 in the old collegiate church at Eton. He sang his first Mass *in Pontificalibus* in the new church, not yet half finished, under a tent erected over the place where the founder had laid the first stone. The approval of the Pope for the establishment of the college was quickly obtained, but Henry desired that the Indulgences granted should be in a more permanent form than that in which they were first granted. These privileges, however ample, were limited to the lifetime of the founder. Writing to Vincent Clement, the King's agent on this matter, Beckynton says: " I would have you

* Rolls Series (*Beckynton Correspondence*), ed. by George Williams, B.D.

believe, that it will be far more acceptable to the King to obtain one moderate *perpetual* indulgence than a great and ample temporary one." There were great delays in obtaining what the King had set his heart upon, and he was very anxious for news. " His daily inquiry is this: " writes the secretary, " When shall we have news of Master Vincent ? When will letters reach us concerning his doings ? " * At length, however, the King's urgent request was satisfied and a Bull, dated 11th May 1444, confirmed the indulgences and privileges previously granted, with the desired clause: " These presents shall continue in force to all future time."

The editor of these letters of Henry VI writes as follows on this matter: " Thus as far as appears from these volumes, the travail pangs of the pious founder in the birth of his college were brought to a happy termination, as regards its spiritual immunities and prerogatives; all destined to be swept ruthlessly away within a century, while the foundation itself, consolidated on a more substantial basis, having survived the storm that wrecked

* Rolls Series (*Beckynton Correspondence*), Introduction, pp. lxxxvi-lxxxvii.

so many other collegiate institutions, abides to this day with a prestige of four centuries of eminent educational success, a worthy monument of the munificent industry of one who, though commonly regarded as the weakest of kings, destitute of all royal and noble qualities, had prescience enough to see that the best remedy for the evils of his age (chiefly created for him by his ambitious uncles and turbulent nobles during his long minority) was to be found in the improved education of all orders of his people; and who, by carrying into effect one grand design, has exercised a more powerful and a more permanent influence over subsequent ages than many princes, whose exploits are the theme of the world's applause "*

The negotiations with Rome regarding Eton were not completed when the same process was repeated on behalf of the King for his foundation of King's College, Cambridge. No fewer than nine of the Bulls obtained for King's College bear dates from 1445 to 1448. "They are interesting," writes Mr. Williams, "as exhibiting the earnest

* Rolls Series (*Beckynton Correspondence*), Introduction, p. lxxxviii.

zeal with which the King prosecuted his great educational designs, and it is abundantly clear that the merit both of the conception and of the execution of those designs belongs in great measure to the youthful sovereign himself."

KING'S COLLEGE CHAPEL, CAMBRIDGE

From an engraving by Loggar

# IV

# TESTIMONY OF CONTEMPORARIES AS TO HENRY'S PERSONALITY AND CHARACTER

IT is important to understand how those who were the contemporaries of King Henry VI, or who come immediately afterwards, regarded his personality. John Ross, the Warwickshire antiquary, who was a contemporary of King Henry and remembered him, as has been already pointed out, when a student at Oxford, thus writes about him:*
" King Henry VI as he grew in age increased also in virtue. He was most devout to God and the Blessed Virgin Mary from his earliest years; but he was little given to the world and the things of the world; leaving those things always to the Council. He founded the new college of Cambridge and that of Eton near Windsor. Moreover, he increased the pos-

* Joannis Rossi, *Hist. Regum Angliae*, ed. Hearne, p. 210.

sessions of New College and of the Royal
College of Oriel at Oxford. He was twice
crowned, as King of England at Westminster,
and then as King of France at Paris. He was
buried twice, and it is believed by many that
he will be buried yet a third time.* This
most holy man was wickedly driven from his
kingdom after the shedding of much blood
in the armed conflicts. He was captured and
put into prison, where he suffered most
patiently for years. A second time regaining
his royal throne, he did not long retain it, but
was again thrust into prison and at last
crowned by martyrdom he was taken into the
everlasting company of God's elect, in a wonderful manner being made known by miracles.
He conquered by his patience, and by this
patience he gave a lesson to all."

CAPGRAVE, also a contemporary of the pious
King Henry, writes of him whilst he was still
alive: " My Lord the King can confidently
expect that He, who has begun a good work,
will perfect it. He willingly attends to the
business of the Kingdom and administers
justice rightly. As in the case of St. Louis it

* This refers to the proposed translation of the body
to Westminster.

may be said of him: ' It is holy and pious and proper to his royal Majesty, to order nothing that is not honest: he judges only according to justice: he orders nothing that is not right: and he first does himself, what he proposes to order others to do.'

" Would that his subjects might only follow the example of our King! With what reverence does he not sign himself with the sign of the cross, when he meets his priests! I know many men in the vigour of life, who never held the cross in much veneration, who by the King's example were brought to a greater fervour and to a more faithful practice of making use of the glorious sign of the cross of Christ. One instance of this may perhaps be not unpleasing to our Lord King as show-ing how his subjects are being reformed by his example. It is said of him—and this is proved by long experience—that he never allowed the Church or ecclesiastics to be molested. Following the example of the great Constantine, he took special delight in pious talks with ecclesiastics. This most devout King Henry, in the nineteenth year of his reign, founded two colleges, and on these works he expended great sums of money and exercised constant personal care over them. He crowned his work by himself laying the first stone, and as I myself [*i.e.* Capgrave] witnessed, he offered this his foundation to God Almighty with the deepest devotion." *

BERNARD ANDRÉ, who wrote in the reign of Henry VII, tells how the pious King Henry VI had foretold the accession of the then king to the English throne; and speaking of the imprisonment of the former, says: " I cannot here keep back my tears, when thinking of the savage, fierce and cruel way in which this holy man was treated." Then after a lamentation upon the excesses of the Wars of the Roses, he says: " This King [Henry VI] always obeyed thy commandments O God! he was always just, pious and innocent. And so at last in regard to this holy King it is made known that he, who was wrongly deposed from his royal throne, is crowned with a celestial diadem, together with the kings in heaven." †

The same contemporary authority, Bernard André, also speaks of the heroic patience of the King in bearing his sufferings in prison.

* *De illustribus Henricis* (Rolls Series), pp. 130-3.
† *Historia Reg. H. VII* (Rolls Series), pp. 14-20.

He gives what he calls a prayer of the saintly monarch whilst in the Tower: " I should be wholly without gratitude, O sweetest Jesus, were I not to give thanks to Thee for my many misfortunes as well as for the good things I have received. Thou knowest what good fortune and what ill fortune Thou hast given me in the course of my life. I have accepted both the good and the bad most willingly from Thy hands, who causest the sun to shine on the good and the wicked and sendest the rain upon the just and unjust. The prosperity Thou hast given me I proclaim not by way of boasting, but in thanksgiving. Thou hast given me royal parents, of a noble and ancient race. This occasion might require me to name the numberless great deeds of my Father in France, but my prayer leads me to other thoughts and this only I say about myself to give the glory to God.

" I was crowned in the prosperous city of Paris, and I later married the chaste daughter of the King of Sicily, a most wise woman, and from her I had a son, Prince Edward. For many years the kingdom was governed in peace. For these things it is better to be grateful than to mourn. And now, though I am overwhelmed by ills of every kind, if I but bear them in patience they will add to my merit. Wherefore whatever by God's will I have to suffer, I will bear. Patience is not too long for those who have sinned. There is no evil in death, except what follows death. Death itself is not to be accounted an evil when it follows on a good life." These and such like thoughts, says André, the King constantly preached to his gaolers.*

Shortly after the accession of King Henry VII the historian, Polydore Vergil, came to England and began to collect materials for his history of England. This work he undertook at the instance of the King himself. He was certainly most diligent in collecting his information about recent events, and consequently what he has to say about the saintly King Henry VI may be taken as almost contemporary evidence. Of the death of the King he writes: " Henry VI, the most innocent of men, having shortly before been despoiled of his Kingdom, was put to death in the Tower. The persistent report is that Richard, Duke of Gloucester, killed him with a sword, so as to free his brother Edward then king from all

* *Historia Reg. H. VII* (Rolls Series), p. 22.

TALBOT, EARL OF SHREWSBURY, PRESENTING A BOOK TO
MARGARET OF ANJOU AND HENRY VI

(MS. Roy. 15, E. VI, c. 1445)

fears of opposition. But, whoever may have been the actual author of the death of this holy man, it appears certain enough that the brothers Edward, Gloucester and the Duke of Clarence gave orders for it. The dead body of Henry was taken from the Tower, without any marks of honour, to St. Paul's Church and was exposed there all day. The next day it was transported to the Monastery of St. Benedict at Chertsey, fifteen miles from London, and there buried. Immediately the tomb began to be celebrated for numerous miracles. Not long after the body was carried away to Windsor Castle and placed in the Church of St. George, where it now [*i.e. circa* 1510] rests and is greatly honoured for many miracles." *

" This King Henry reigned thirty-eight years, and after recovering his kingdom, again, for another six months more. He lived to the age of fifty-two. He was tall of stature: his body was slender and his members in every way corresponded; his face was comely, and it ever reflected the bountiful goodness of the disposition with which he was abundantly endowed. By natural disposition he was

* *MS. Vat. Urb. Lat.*, 198(1), fol. 205 *seqq.*

opposed to every vice both of body and soul, from which, even from his tender youth, he kept himself free. He was pure and clean of mind; partook of no evil; ready to embrace all that was good. He had a contempt of all those things which commonly corrupt the minds of men. So patient also was he in suffering injuries and insults received from his enemies, that he never sought to revenge them, but for the very same gave God Almighty his most humble thanks, because by them he trusted that his sins might be washed away. Indeed—this good, gracious, holy, sober and wise man would declare that all these miseries had happened to him on account of his own and of his ancestors manifold offences. Wherefore he did not think of any dignity or honour, or State or of the son or friends he had lost, or make 'much dole' for them. But if in anything he had offended God, this he thought of, for this he mourned, for this he was sorry.

"These and such like acts and practices of perfect holiness caused God for his sake to manifest many miracles in his lifetime. Even to-day many are still living, who have witnessed these miracles and testified to their

exiſtence, and *they are everywhere known!* *
For this reason King Henry VII, not without
cause, began a few years ago to try and pro-
cure his canonization as a saint from the
Supreme Pontiff, Pope Julius II. But he was
prevented by death from prosecuting that
honourable cause,† and left it to his son,
Henry VIII, to accomplish.

"Moreover Henry [VI] had a moſt liberal
mind. He held good learning in great
reverence and loved those who were endued
with it. For this reason he helped his own
people to obtain proper teaching. He founded
a sumptuous school at Eton, a town adjoining
Windsor. In this, he eſtablished a college of
prieſts and a great number of children to be
educated there and taught their grammar free
and without coſt. In the same way he was the
founder of King's College at Cambridge,
which at this day [*c.* 1510] so flourishes and
with such ornaments of learning that it may
well be called the Prince of all Colleges." ‡

* *MS. Vat. Urb. Lat.*, 198(1), fol. 206. This last
clause, taken from the original draft of the history, is
left out in the printed edition.

† This last part "and left," etc., is also left out in
the printed edition.

‡ *MS. Vat. Urb. Lat.*, 198(1), fol. 206.

JOHN STOW, the chronicler, can vouch for the ordinary opinion of England regarding King Henry VI in the latter half of the sixteenth century. In his *Annals* (ed. 1592) he thus writes: " The one and twentieth of May, King Edward came to London with 30,000 men, and the same night King Henry was murdered in the Tower of London. On the morrow he was brought to St. Paules Church in London, in an open coffin barefaced, where he bled: thence he was carried to the Black Friars and he bled: and thence to Chertsey Abbey in a boat, where he was buried, but since removed to Windsor where he was buried without the chancel at the south door of the choir of Windsor Chapel. Here he was worshipped by the name of holy King Henry: whose red hat of velvet was thought to heal the headache of such as should put it on their heads. There he rested for a time, but now his tomb being taken thence it is not (commonly) known what is become of his body."

" Thus ended the King's transitory life: having enjoyed as great prosperity as favourable fortune could afford, and as great troubles on the other side, as she frowning could pour out. Yet in both states he was patient and virtuous, that he may be considered a pattern of most perfect virtue, as he was a worthy exemplar of fortune's inconsistency.* He was plain, upright, fair from fraud, wholly given to prayer, reading of [the] Scriptures and Almsdeeds; of such integrity of life that the Bishop, who had been his confessor for ten years, avouched that he had not all that time committed any mortal crime. So continent, as suspicion of such in life never touched him. . . . He was so religiously affected (as the time was then) that on principal holy days he would wear sackcloth next his skin. . . . He was of seemly stature, of body slender, his face beautiful, of his own natural inclination, he abhorred all the vices as well of the body as of the soul."

An old historical " chart of English History," now in the English College, Rome, written in the reign of King Henry VIII, whom it describes as the present King (*modernus rex*), says of Henry VI: " This King was most holy during the whole of his life,

* Much of the account given by Stow is obviously taken from Blackman's life, although it is not named as his authority.

and after death was renowned for some miracles. For this reason Henry VII took care to refer to the Roman Pontiff that he might be added to the number of the Saints."

There can be little doubt as to the reputation for sanctity which the murdered King possessed in the popular mind from the first. It will be necessary to speak more at length of the *cultus* and devotion generally accorded to him.   Here it will be useful to take only one or two examples: At York Minster, as early as 1473, there already had been placed a statue of the King on the choir screen; and this was still there in 1516, in spite of the prohibition of the King and the Archbishop.  The editor of the Fabric Rolls of York Minster,* in recording this fact, says: "Though not canonized he [King Henry VI] was certainly regarded as a saint by many of his adherents. His many virtues, his gentleness of character, and his many misfortunes endeared him to a great portion of his subjects.  Dean Alexander, who erected the statue, knew him well, having been his private secretary."

It is of course obvious that such a manifestation of popular devotion must have been

* Surtees Soc., vol. xxxv, p. 79.

eminently distasteful to the two kings, Edward IV and Richard III—the one who had supplanted him and the one who, as all the people believed, had been his murderer. It was probably through the royal influence that in 1479 Archbishop Bothe of York issued his monition against the reverence shown to the saintly King in the Minster, on the ground that such honour was unlawful until the approbation of the Sovereign Pontiff had been obtained. This, however, did not put an end to the very general devotion to the King, and as the same editor writes: " There were few towns of any consequence in England in which an image of the King was not erected in the principal church. There was one at Ripon and another at Durham, to take only a couple of instances in the north, whilst in the east of England (an image) was, and indeed is still, to be seen in many altar screens."

The testimony of NICHOLAS HARPESFIELD is of great importance as to the popular devotion to Henry VI. Harpesfield wrote his work, *Historia Ecclesiastica Anglicana*,\* when in prison for his religion in the reign of

\* Published 1621.

Elizabeth. He had been Archdeacon of Canterbury, and this position, till deprived of his office for his religious beliefs, enabled him to obtain first-hand information on the matters of which he treats. And the authorities he cites in the course of his narrative prove that he could deal as an historian with evidence in a masterly way. Moreover, he had access, when gathering his material, to such important documents as the Episcopal Registers of Canterbury and elsewhere.

In his general History * Harpesfield writes about the life and character of the saintly King Henry as follows: " He was a man of modest, straightforward, and mild disposition. He detested war, and his true desire was to devote himself in quiet and peace to divine meditation and study. He was ever watchful and careful. He did not oppress his people by excessive taxation or by exacting tributes. His patience under overwhelming troubles was evident. He never desired to take reprisals, nor did he seek vengeance, but he accepted everything from God's hands, taking these misfortunes as sent him to punish his own sins and those of his ancestors. His life

* *Hist. Anglicana,* p. 593.

was ever most innocent: and this was allowed even by his enemies and is attested by miracles.

"Henry in the course of his life passed many laws in favour of religion. Amongst others he decreed that no markets or fairs were to be held on Sundays, or on the great feasts of our Lord and the Saints, or on Good Friday. On such days he ordered his people to abstain from all work and especially to guard against perpetrating frauds, committing perjury, or uttering falsehoods, etc."

In a later section of his *Historia* Harpesfield speaks at length as to the well-known miracles which attested the sanctity of this holy King. He heads this chapter with the words: "Regarding the Miracles of King Henry VI after his death; of their frequent occurrence and of their no less certainty and truth."* He begins by referring again to the King's life, which was full of troubles and difficulties; but which he bore so patiently to the great increase of his eternal glory. That Henry was placed in a high place in heaven is, in the author's opinion, proved by the miracles, which were worked by him and through his intercession after his death. "Apart from the document-

* *Hist. Anglicana*, p. 595.

ary proofs," he says, " I would easily believe them, because of the exceptional virtues he displayed in his life. His father, Henry V, was indeed honoured by all posterity by reason of his great deeds, but much greater and much more celebrated was his son [Henry VI], if only by reason of the wonders worked by his intercession after his death. After his abominable murder, he was buried in the Benedictine monastery of Chertsey, and there, after a few years, he became renowned throughout England for the great miracles wrought at his tomb. So, whether for this reason, or through the guilty conscience of him by whose advice and even by whose hand he was murdered, or, as I readily believe, by divine inspiration Richard [III] caused the body of the blessed King to be transferred to Windsor. And, although he was known already for many and great miracles, after his body had been transferred to the place of his birth, his fame for these wonders increased in such a marvellous way, that hardly a day passed without someone coming to render thanks to him for some cure, which had been considered to be beyond human help, from which he had suffered or been burdened, and from which he had been freed at that place. Sometimes on the same day many people arrived together for this purpose at Windsor. And these miracles were indeed so clear and so well known, that Henry VII petitioned Pope Julius II to add the name of the holy King to the catalogue of the Saints. It is believed that these demands would have been successful, had not the King's death intervened. Indeed, this was not the only time Henry VII had urged his petition, as it appears he had already done so in the time of Alexander VI." "I know not why the matter was delayed in this manner ... but whatever the reason the miracles of Henry were so absolutely credited and their certainty was so clear that I would readily believe that had Henry VII not died prematurely, or had others afterwards taken any pains in the matter, the decree of the Church would have been granted.

" These miracles were set down in writing with every detail set forth with great accuracy, and committed to writing in English, by the care and diligence of John Morgan, Dean of the college of Windsor, who afterwards became Bishop of Menaevia, and by Oliver King, a Canon of the Church of Windsor, afterwards designated Bishop of Exeter; and other Canons of the Church helped them. Later the greater part of the relation was translated into Latin by a pious and learned monk at the Dean's request. The monk's name is not known to me [Harpesfield] with certainty. But I came upon this translation, after having myself made a long enquiry into these miracles. This monk collected and described not indeed all the miracles, but some two hundred more or less. The collection forms a goodly volume, and it would seem as if the translation was made so as to be sent to the Supreme Pontiff and the Cardinals, in order that they might have solid and mature grounds for enrolling King Henry among the Saints. Whether it was ever sent to Rome I cannot yet say for certain; but anyone who reads the volume can have no hesitation in believing in the truth of these miracles. The author [of the above-named] has done his work so wonderfully well that he has not left out the name of any person whom the holy King's intercession has delivered from some ill or misfortune, nor the place where he lived, nor the time, nor indeed any other circumstances connected with the matter."

Harpesfield then says that in the church at Windsor there were shown great numbers of votive offerings, testifying to the graces there received through the intercession of the saintly King. These included sticks and crutches of all kinds, used by people who had been cured there, and who, returning without them, left them as a testimony of their gratitude to God. There were also innumerable waxen images of various members of the human body—eyes, hands, feet, etc., models of the afflicted parts —which had been cured by the intercession of King Henry. " I note in this volume," continues the author, " that there were many of these people who, after having been cured, made an exact relation concerning it, also that those who had derived any benefit furnished the sworn testimony of those that were present when the miracle took place. In regard to many cases no enquiry could be carried out either because the subject had since died or could not be traced."

" There was no diocese, no province, no city nor town; no village or even country side in England in which there was not reported fresh instances of cures and favours and other benefits, obtained by the intercession of

Henry. From the far western parts of England and from the extreme north of the country, not to speak of places which are near at hand, there came bands of pilgrims proclaiming aloud the help which they had obtained from this holy King."

The author then goes on to picture the number of the pilgrims who flocked to the shrine at Windsor. He speaks at length of cures of all sorts worked by Henry's intercession, of the freedom obtained from all manner of troubles, and of relief from misfortune of every kind obtained at his tomb. It is quite impossible, he declares, to set down all the numberless and marvellous cures effected in a few years by this wonder worker. They are so many and so various that a mere list would be lengthy and difficult to compile, if not beyond human power and industry. The blind, the lame, the dumb, the deaf, lunatics, and those possessed by evil spirits obtained relief. People injured by the unexpected falling of earth upon them, etc. Others suffering from wounds beyond the cure of doctors and surgeons; others suffocating by bones, etc., which had lodged in their throats and which no human skill had been able to extract; others in peril of shipwreck or of drowning in mill dams or in the sea; others afflicted by the plague, by virulent ulcers, by toothache or headache, colic and, in a word, by all manner of diseases only a few of which could be recorded, and whose lot was deplored by their friends and their doctors; others who had fallen from tree tops and the roofs of houses and had thus been almost broken to pieces; those struck by lightning; those burning with St. Anthony's fire, etc. These and numberless other cases of illness and disease received relief through the intercession of the holy King from the hand of God.

But more than this: not only ills of this kind were cured, but in several cases where life itself was extinct, it was restored through the King's intercession before the throne of God. This is attested in the Book of the Saint's miracles in several cases. Amongst others there is cited the case of two innocent men who were hanged at Salisbury and at Cambridge, the truth of which cases is attested by the Bishops of Salisbury, Ely, and Chichester; also there is given the case of a priest whose sight and speech were restored to him. " When," says Harpesfield, " I think of these wonders, I seem to see him [King Henry VI] again on his royal throne, no less powerful than of old or less desirous of administering justice than when he was vested with his royal power." To take one or two other instances: a girl named Agnes Freeman in Kent was seriously attacked by the King's evil, which was considered to be incurable. Her friends urged that she should be taken to King Richard, who then occupied the throne; but her parents, following better advice, implored the assistance of King Henry, vowing to make a pilgrimage to his tomb. Directly the vow was made a change for the better took place, and in three or four days she was perfectly cured.

In another part of his History Harpesfield records how, at the execution of an innocent man, the blessed King Henry appeared and prevented the rope, by which he was being hanged, from strangling him; and this man lived to thank God for the grace given him through the saintly King. The author also notes that after death, Henry often appeared to suppliants in corporal form, vested in his royal robes. In one case a certain Richard Boys, of West Harptree, five miles or so from Bath, was condemned to death for a crime of which he was innocent. He appealed to the protection of our Lady and the blessed King, and was saved from execution at the laſt moment. He made a pilgrimage to the shrine at Windsor and left there the rope, with which he was to have been hanged, as a teſtimony of his indebtedness to the intercession of the holy King. This man was accompanied to Windsor on this visit of thanksgiving by forty of his fellow townsmen, and they went also afterwards to Walsingham to return thanks to our Blessed Lady.

Finally, to give another inſtance of the wonders worked by the King shortly after his death, a man named Fuller, of Hammersmith, was condemned to death for having been accidentally in the company of a band of criminals when they were captured. As the King during his life had always been known for his juſtice, this poor man craved his intercession, and he was ultimately set free. Fuller made a pilgrimage to the tomb of the King when his body was ſtill at Chertsey, and he paid his devotion there on the very day before the body was carried away to Windsor. Subsequently he went to Windsor to thank the holy King again for his intercession before the throne of God. A passing reference to the pilgrimages and the devotion to the saintly King which continued long after the forcible destruction of his shrine at Windsor is to be found in pages of Foxe the " Martyrologist." In 1543 this writer gives an account of the " Trouble and Persecution of Four Wyndsormen," one Robert Textwood, we are told " as he beheld the pilgrims of Devonshire and Cornwall, how they came in by plums, with candles and images of wax in their hands, to offer to good King Henry of Wyndsor, as they called him, could not refrain to see such great idolatrie committed, and how vainly the people had spent their goods in coming so far to kiss a spur and have an old hat set upon their heads." *

Like other sixteenth-century historians, Speed borrows much of his account of the reign of Henry VI from the narrative of Blackman. After giving a relation of the King's death and burial, Speed adds an appreciation of the character of the monarch. He writes: " Thus lived and thus died this

---

* Foxe, *Book of Martyrs* (1846), v, 467, quoted by Mr. Leonard Smith (*Dublin Review*, 1921).

innocent and just King, who had been proclaimed in his cradle, crowned in his infancy,
and again, at more age had had the Imperial
Diadem of France set on his head, living
uprightly, loving his subjects, and reigning
thirtie eight yeeres, was in that time tossed
with variable successe: for twice he was
imprisoned and deprived of his Crowne,
betrayed, smitten and wounded, and in all
things became a worthy example of fortune's
inconstancy. He was of stature very seemely,
of body slender, of face beautifull, and by a
natural inclination abhorred all vice, farre
from pride, given to prayer, well-read in the
Scriptures, using works of Charitie, and so
chaste, as no suspition of incontinency could
be conceived in him: nay, so farre the contrary,
that when certain Ladies presented themselves
before him in a Maske, with their Haire loose,
and their Brests uncovered (hee then a Bache-
lour and able of marriage) he immediately rose
up and departed the Presence, saying: ' Fie,
fie, forsooth ye are to blame.' Oath he used
none, but in weighty matters, his affirmation
was forsooth, and forsooth; very mercyfull to
the poor, and so pitifull to malefactors, as he
commanded the quarters of traitors to be

taken down from the Gates, and buried, and so farre from revenge that he willingly pardoned the greatest offences against him; for a Ruffian intending his death, wounded him in the side with his Sword, what time he lay a prisoner in the Tower, and being restored to his kingly estate, he freely forgave the fact; and another like Ruffian striking him on the face, he punished with this only reprehension: ' Forsooth you are to blame to strike me, your anointed King ': for these and his other patient vertues, King Henry the Seventh assayed to have him canonized a Saint, but Pope Julius the Second demanding too great a summe, the King went no further in the suite: notwithstanding in the repute of the vulgar he was taken for no less, so as his red Hat which he had worne, healed the headache when it was put on, as the simple beleeved."

# V

# KING HENRY VII PETITIONS FOR THE CANONIZATION OF THE HOLY KING HENRY VI

IN view of the general opinion in England as to the sanctity of the pious King Henry, and of the miracles so constantly worked at his tomb by his intercession, it is not surprising that before the close of the fifteenth century steps were taken to petition for his solemn canonization by the Holy See. From the document about to be quoted it appears that in the Pontificate of Pope Innocent VIII, probably about the year 1490, King Henry VII made his first petition for the canonization. Probably the death of Innocent VIII rendered necessary a second petition, and so in October 1494 Pope Alexander VI issued two Apostolic Letters at the request of King Henry VII, addressed to the Archbishop of Canterbury, Cardinal Morton, and to the Bishop of Durham. The first was to commission these prelates to enquire into matters connected with the canonization of St. Anselm,* and the second, of the same date, to hold a full enquiry into the asserted sanctity and miracles of Henry VI. From this second letter it appears that the King had sent a formal petition for the appointment of a commission to take evidence, in view of the popularly desired canonization. "From the letters of our beloved son in Christ, Henry VII, the illustrious King of England," the Pope writes, "and also from common report, we understand that Henry VI, King of England, of illustrious memory, when he lived on this earth, was well known for the sanctity of his life, for his eminent moral qualities, for his fervent charity to his neighbours, and for every virtue and for all holiness. Moreover, he assiduously practised fasting and continency and was given to prayer and to works of mercy. Also he built, founded, and endowed two great and well-known colleges in England for the education and support of poor scholars, dedicated to the honour of God Almighty and of his glorious Mother. Further, whilst in this life and also after his death the Lord,

* Wilkins, *Concilia*, iii, 641.

through his merits and by his intercession, wrought many and obvious miracles, which continue to this day [1494]. For which people flock with great devotion to his tomb, where the blind are made to see, the deaf to hear, the lame to walk, and those suffering from every kind of infirmity are said to receive relief and health through the power of God, at the intercession of the late King. The fame of all this is widely spread, not only throughout the whole of the said Kingdom, but also in neighbouring lands. Furthermore, a large number of people from other countries are having recourse to him, extraordinary devotion is manifested, and by God's will is ever increasing, so that the absolute belief of the people of these parts is that the name of the said Henry deserved to be inscribed in the catalogue of the Saints.

" For this reason the present King Henry has humbly petitioned Us that some of the prelates of those parts should be commissioned diligently and prudently to enquire into his life, merits, miracles and other of the aforesaid matters and make a faithful report in writing of what they find, so that in Our apostolic benignity We may be pleased to provide what is needful for the canonization of the said late King. Therefore wishing to do what the present King asks, and relying upon the divine judgment rather than upon Our human reason, and likewise desiring to act in a matter of such importance and gravity, We, inclining to the prayer of King Henry and following in the footsteps of Pope Innocent VIII of happy memory, who issued a similar commission, We by these apostolic letters commit to you [the abovenamed prelates] the duty of going personally to Windsor, where the body of the said Henry rests, and of enquiring into his life, merits, sanctity, charity, devotion to God, and his good works, etc. Also to examine into the miracles he wrought during life and after death, etc., calling witnesses to give evidence under oath, as to the ground of their knowledge regarding these things. You are then to report to Us under your hands and seals."*

In the same year, 1494, there is entered in the Episcopal Register of Cardinal Morton of Canterbury a long document setting forth what is necessary to be done in every process of canonization. This almost certainly would appear to have reference to the process to be

* Wilkins, *Concilia*, iii, 640.

instituted in England for the proposed canonization of Henry VI, and for this reason is of
interest and importance. The document in
question sets forth at great length the various
steps which have to be taken and the enquiries
which have to be made into the life and virtues
of the person proposed for canonization, and
then into the miracles which are said to have
been worked, and for which evident proof has
to be forthcoming. Then follows in the
document an account of the ceremonies in
Rome, together with the fees and costs of a
public canonization.*

This official paper partly helps us to understand the delay which took place in the process of the canonization of King Henry, for
it says that when some person of authority
approaches the Roman Pontiff in such a
matter, not once but many times *instantes
instancius*, the Pope does not act at once, but
waits till the reputation of sanctity grows and
miracles are claimed as having happened and
have been proved by tested evidence. All
this is the work of the preliminary enquiries
made in the country and place where the
proposed saint lived. If the demand for the

* Wilkins, *Concilia*, iii, 636-9.

canonization continues to be urged, and if the
fame of sanctity and the miracles still persist,
then the Roman Pontiff issues a commission
to certain bishops or other responsible people
in the country to hold a full enquiry into the
reputed sanctity and the devotion of the
people, and into the miracles, etc.  The prelates so commissioned have to report as to the
general evidence, and not as to specific cases,
as to the general and common reputation, and
not as to the truth or ground of the belief.
The particulars were to be left for another
enquiry into the truth of the alleged facts.
After the report of the first commission had
been made to Rome, the Pontiff would
determine by the advice of his officials
whether the second enquiry was to be ordered
or not.  If it was ordered to be undertaken,
the same bishops or others were to be directed
to take evidence in regard to the *truth* of the
reputation of the sanctity of life of the servant
of God, and as to the evidence for the miracles
alleged to have been worked.  When this
had been done the commissioners were to
send to the Pope the result of their enquiry,
with all the evidence collected.

In the same year (1494) that Pope Alexander VI issued his commission of enquiry " into the truth of the facts " of the sanctity of Henry VI and of miracles attributed to his intercession, King Henry VII made petition to the Pope to be allowed to transfer the body of the saintly monarch from Windsor to Westminster Abbey. This the Pope allowed, and in his Bull granting the permission he recites the grounds upon which the royal petition was based. Henry VII had assured him, he says, that the holy King, his uncle, after having been deprived of his kingdom, had been buried away in a remote place like Chertsey and placed in a tomb unworthy of such a monarch. When, " in course of time it pleased Almighty God to manifest the holiness of this King by miracles, and people began to come to his tomb with their offerings, Richard III, who then occupied the throne, and who had pursued the holy man with his hatred whilst alive, and whose brutal nature and malignity had eradicated all feelings of affection and humanity, envying the public veneration of Henry and the concourse of people to his tomb, in order to put a stop to this manifestation of devotion, caused his holy body to be dug up and buried in the

Collegiate Church of Windsor Castle, where at present his body, bones, and relics rest." Now, however, the Abbot and Convent of Westminster claim that the Abbey Church is the only fitting place for his tomb. It is the place where the Kings of England are crowned and in which many of them lie buried. It is also the place where the chief nobles of the kingdom meet, which is most frequently visited by Englishmen, and which is best known by other nations. Henry VII, therefore, prays the Pope " to permit the translation of his relics to this monastery of Westminster, where they may rest near to the tomb of his parents at a spot to which the ever-increasing crowds of pilgrims may conveniently come, and thus help the religious sentiments of the country and render more famous the merits of this holy man."*

Meanwhile, however, it would appear that Henry VII had not fully made up his mind about the translation of the relics from Windsor. In the same year, 1494, he had applied to the Pope † for leave to suppress the two religious houses of Mottisfont in Hampshire

* Wilkins, *Concilia*, iii, 635.
† Rymer, *Foedera*, vii, 563.

and Suffield in Buckinghamshire, and to apply
their endowments to the building of a new
chantry and hospital at Windsor in which he
himself proposed to be buried, and where he
intended to erect a shrine over the relics of
Henry VI. Even in view of the future translation to Westminster it seems evident that
there was no intention of abandoning the idea
of the chantry, etc., at Windsor, for in 1494
and the following years various Papal Bulls
granted the indulgences of the *Scala Sancta* to
the proposed building.

There were, moreover, difficulties in the
way of the proposed translation to Westminster, and Mr. Leonard Smith, in an interesting article on the *Canonization of Henry VI*
in the *Dublin Review* * states these as follows.
"In 1498 a controversy arose before the Privy
Council, between the Abbot of Chertsey, the
Dean of Windsor, and the Abbot of Westminster as to who was entitled to the possession of the relics which it was now proposed to
exhume a second time. Each of the rival
claimants appeared in person, with documents
and witnesses to make good his claim. The
Abbot of Chertsey for his part affirmed that he

* January 1921.

had never consented to the removal of the body to Windsor in 1484, and that, therefore, since it had been taken from his keeping unlawfully, he was now entitled to its recovery. The Dean of Windsor and his supporters argued that so far from having objected to the exhumation, the Abbot of Chertsey with his own hands had assisted thereat, and that inasmuch as the dead King had declared his wish to be interred at Windsor, and was in fact now buried there, the body should remain where it was. The Abbot of Westminster, however, put forward the most convincing arguments. Four volumes of evidence were presented in his behalf, and numerous witnesses—vergers, servants, and workmen of the Abbey—deposed to the frequent visits paid by Henry VI to the Abbey at all hours of the day and night during the fateful years of 1458-1461, and described how he had chosen a burial-place for himself there, near to the tomb of his father, King Henry V, and of Queen Catherine his mother. The Abbot further urged the close connection that had always existed between the Abbey and the Royal Palace of Westminster, and laid stress upon the fact that during his lifetime the dead King had

been the Abbey's parishioner.  On 5th March
1498 judgement was accordingly given by
the Privy Council in favour of the Abbot of
Westminster in the presence of the King, and
in July following, an Indenture was drawn up
between the King and George Fawcett,
Abbot of Westminster, whereby the Abbot,
the Prior, and the Convent bound themselves
to pay the sum of five hundred pounds, by
three yearly instalments, towards the expenses
of the translation of the body from Windsor
to Westminster.  This sum was in fact paid,
as the accounts of John Islip, Sacrist of Westminster, for 1501 prove."  Meanwhile steps
had been taken to supply the Commission
charged by Alexander VI with the examination of the cause, with a body of evidence
relating to the miracles alleged to have been
worked at Henry's intercession.  At a date
not much later than the close of the year 1500,
a manuscript translation into Latin* of two
books of miracles of King Henry VI already
existing in English was made by an unknown
writer at the request of Dean Morgan of
Windsor.  The writer implies that this com-
pilation of four separate collections of miracles,

* B.M. Royal MS. 13, c. viii.

in many cases with minute details of persons, circumstances, and times, had been undertaken in order that it might be submitted to the judgement of ecclesiastical authority; and from the marginal annotations in another contemporary hand — " probatum," " nullius effectus," " non reperitur," " non probatum," —it is clear that an attempt to weigh the evidence was in fact made. The earliest miracle recorded is assigned to 1481; the last is dated July 1500.

The permission granted by Pope Alexander VI for the translation of the body of Henry VI to Westminster was not acted upon at the time, and in 1502 King Henry VII began to prepare for the building of the celebrated chapel at Westminster which goes by his name. The foundation stone was laid " at a quarter of an houre afore three of the clock, at afternoon " on 24th January 1503. He intended that it should contain the body of his saintly predecessor, and in fact the shrine that he prepared for the relics remains to attest his veneration and his firm expectation that his petition for Henry's canonization would most certainly be ultimately granted.

Time went on, and for one reason or another

the work of the Commission to enquire into
the sanctity of the holy King Henry VI was
delayed. Cardinal Morton died in 1500, and
his fellow Commissioner, the Bishop of
Durham, followed him to the grave in 1501.
The Cardinal had arrived at a great age, and
during many years was mostly so occupied in
the affairs of State that he could have found
little time to attend to the business of the
Papal Commission. In Rome Pope Alexander VI died in 1503, and after the brief
reign of Pius III, he was succeeded by Pope
Julius II. It was consequently necessary to
have recourse once more to Rome, and so, the
year after Pope Julius's succession, Henry VII
once again sent another petition for the canonization of his saintly predecessor, which was
couched in almost identical terms as those of
the former demand of 1494. This new petition was forthwith granted by Pope Julius II,
and the then Archbishop of Canterbury,
Archbishop Warham, was associated with
the Bishops of Winchester, Durham, and
London in the Commission of enquiry
appointed in 1504.*

At the same time Henry VII again applied

* *Arch. Vat. Reg. Lat.*, 984, fol. 49.

to the new Pope for permission to translate the
body of the saintly Henry VI to Westminster.
This was again granted in 1504,* by which
time the Chapel intended to receive the relics
was already making progress.   Three years
later, in 1507, Archbishop Warham and the
three Bishops of Winchester, Durham, and
London, who had been appointed to make the
enquiry into the life and miracles of Henry VI,
petitioned Pope Julius II to be allowed to
appoint delegates to take the necessary
evidence at Windsor and elsewhere.   They
pleaded that some of the witnesses to be
examined in England and in other lands, by
reason of their old age and infirmities, were
unable to present themselves to give their
testimony, and that it was consequently
necessary to make provision for their examination.   The King of England, Henry VII, also
urged this necessity.   Wherefore, writes the
Pope, in his reply, " We, thinking that it is
not right to leave without the due veneration
of men, one whom the Almighty has raised
to Heaven," grant the faculty asked for, and
allow you to appoint worthy prelates to go to

* *Arch. Vat. Reg. Lat.*, 984, fol. 53.

the places where such witnesses are to be found and there take the evidence. "They are to examine these witnesses and to transmit to Us their findings and the whole processes testified by their private seals." *

It would appear that this examination was still in progress when King Henry VII died in 1509. There is no evidence to show that the necessary documents were ever sent to Rome subsequently, although, according to the testimony of Polydore Vergil, King Henry VII left it as a charge to his son, Henry VIII, to carry out the canonization, which he had not succeeded in obtaining during his life. As far as can be ascertained this charge was neglected, and early in the reign of the eighth Henry it became evident that he was not likely to respect these wishes of his father, and later, of course, the sequence of events in the quarrel with the Holy See, and the various attacks of the Reformation principles on the *cultus* of the Saints put an end to the case altogether. At first, however, Henry VIII appears to have intended to carry out the wishes of his father, at least in regard to the

* *Arch. Vat. Reg. Lat.,* 1204, fol. 228.

translation of the relics of the holy King to Westminster. According to the will of Henry VII, made in the last year of his life, his successor was urged " to translate right shortly " to Westminster " the body and relics of our Uncle of blessed memory, King Henry the VIth." Almost twenty years after the death of Henry VII, namely in 1528 —the year before the fall of Wolsey—the idea of securing the canonization does not appear to have been entirely given up. The King's Ambassadors to the Holy See, D. Gardiner Fox, the royal almoner, and Sir Gregory de Cassalis, then engaged in the matter of the King's divorce, wrote to Cardinal Wolsey from Orvieto, in regard to the proposed canonization as follows: " We have moved the Pope's holiness as towching the Canonization of K. Henry VI, who answerith that he is very well content to make schort process therein; but the matiers must be examyned here, requiring a number of Cardinals therat, with other ceremonies, which cannot be done there. Wherefore yf my Lord of Canterbury and my Lord of Winchester, who have examyned the matier *in partibus* do send the process hither as their commission requyred, the sentence of canonization shal schortly pass here." *

It is of interest to note that at the end of his reign King Henry VIII still had a religious devotion to the saintly King Henry VI. In his will he directs " that at our expense the tomb and altar of King Henry VI be made more magnificent in the place where it is at present."

* Brewer, *Letters, etc., of King Henry VIII*, iv, no. 4167.

# THE RELATIONS OF HENRY VI WITH THE CHURCH AND POPE

IT is useful to understand the attitude of the saintly King Henry towards the Church and its supreme head, the Pope. His letters, as they appear in the Beckynton correspondence, manifest an extraordinary and constant desire to serve the best interests of the Church of Christ, and a devotion and filial reverence for the Supreme Pontiff. It has already been pointed out how eager he was to obtain Pope Eugenius' approval for his two colleges of Eton and Cambridge, and how he pressed him to give them perpetuity by extending the original Indulgences beyond the term of his own life as founder, to which the privileges had been limited at first. This attitude manifests the King's belief in the Catholic doctrine of indulgences, and his understanding that the papal approval was necessary to secure the purpose he had in view in founding these two great English educational establishments.

In connection with these two colleges there is a clause in the instructions he gave to his envoys sent to the Council of Basle, which is of importance. It deals with a question which the King thought might be raised at that assembly in regard to the alienation of certain estates in England formerly belonging to the alien priories. In this document the seizure of this alien property is justified, writes the editor of this correspondence, " on the ground of public policy and by the consideration of the abuse of the revenues to anti-national purposes, during the wars with France." *
It is, moreover, asserted that his father, King Henry V, instead of appropriating these revenues to his own private uses, as he might lawfully have done, had applied for and procured permission from Pope Martin V to convert them to the endowment of monasteries and churches and other pious purposes, as, in fact, he had done. At the same time he made liberal compensation to the churches and monasteries in France and the Duchy of Normandy for any losses they may have

* *Beckynton Correspondence*, Introd., p. lxxxix.

sustained by the diversion of the revenues
derivable from their possessions in England.
It was consequently in prosecution of his
father's design, and with due papal licence,
that Henry VI assigned the revenues of some
of the suppressed alien houses to the endowment of his new colleges. The preservation
of the religious character of these revenues
was secured by grafting the educational establishments on to collegiate churches of secular
priests, which mixed character Eton still
retains.*

In 1433 Henry condemns the independent
attitude of the Council of Basle in strong
terms. He protests against the language of
the assembly regarding the Pope, which has
shocked the minds of the faithful. " In the
sacred Synod," he says, " some people lacking
in all modesty had given free rein to their
ungoverned tongues, and have uttered unworthy, indecent, and injurious words against
Our Holy Father the Lord Eugenius, the
supreme Pontiff of the Universal Church.
They, the sheep, have irreverently attacked
the Shepherd; being sons, they have raised
their heads against their father; being sub-

* *Beckynton Correspondence*, Introd., p. lxxxix.

jects they have despised and rebelled against their head. And what we marvel at more is that they have set aside the present hope for peace and concord between the Lord Eugenius and themselves, for which the Roman Emperor and other lovers of peace will not cease to work, and which, as far as possible, We are determined to labour for in conjunction with other princes and ecclesiastics who desire it." *

In a letter which King Henry wrote at this time to Theodore, Archbishop of Cologne, he tells him that he is devoting himself heart and soul to the work of securing peace and union, which is so necessary for the Church and for the whole world, and he gladly includes in this the peace between England and France. He has long and earnestly laboured, he says, for the peace of the Church, and there is nothing he more desires.

He addressed the Emperor Sigismund in the same sense, imploring him to prevent the schism threatened at Basle. He laments the evil treatment of the Pope by those who, in spite of the closure of the Council and the protests of the Cardinals present, had deter-

* *Beckynton Correspondence*, p. 65.

mined to continue their meetings. It is, he says, the plain duty of Christian princes to prevent this evil, and he trusts the Emperor to act, and he himself desires to co-operate to stop this schismatical action.*

In his zeal for the Catholic faith King Henry took much to heart this disobedient attitude of the Council of Basle towards Pope Eugenius IV. By his Bull *Doctoris gentium* in September 1537, the Supreme Pontiff declared the Council ended, and later transferred it to Ferrara. The Fathers at Basle, or, rather, some of them, refused to recognize the right of the Pope to do this, and they desired to continue their discussions in spite of him. On reports of this action reaching the King, he addressed a strong letter of expostulation to the recalcitrant Fathers. He deplored their attitude, which must bring grief and dismay to all faithful sons of the Church. He begs them to pause and consider what they are doing in actually citing " the most Holy father and lord Eugenius, a man who from his youth onward has ever enjoyed the reputation of holiness and modesty, and who possesses every moral quality to make him the pious

* *Beckynton Correspondence*, p. 84.

H

upright pastor of the Church, which he certainly is. The attitude of the Council towards the Pope," he says, " is a direct perversion of the order established by Christ. ' What the Vicar of Christ binds, you endeavour to loose, what he looses you desire to bind; what he thinks well to open you endeavour to shut up, etc.' By the waves of this discord you cause the bark of Peter to be tossed about hither and thither." *

He writes also to the Pope in the same strain of grave anxiety, begging him by every means to put an end at once to the dissensions, which will lead to a schism.† It endangers the possible union of the Greeks with the West, which he ardently desires. He himself has spared no pains in this matter and has written to the Emperor and the Imperial electors to beg them to extend their authority and, if necessary, their arms to avert this schism.‡

Henry's appeals to the obstinate contingent at Basle had no effect: they were indeed treated with arrogant protests and disdain. On hearing this, he wrote again in May 1438, saying that this treatment in no wise has

* *Beckynton Correspondence*, ii, 37-45.
† *Ibid.*, p. 46.          ‡ *Ibid.*

turned his mind or his will from the "zeal of filial devotion, reverence and affection, with which, following in the footsteps of my predecessors, as a devoted son of the Church, I intend to uphold all who labour for Holy Mother Church and its prosperity and peace." He desires nothing more on earth than peace, and he prays that the grace of the Holy Spirit may inspire and enlighten the minds and hearts of the Fathers at Basle to help to calm the dangerous storm and to assist in bringing the bark of Peter into a port of safety.*

In 1438 the Pope convoked the Council of Florence, and the following year the English King expressed himself delighted to hear that the union of the Greeks had been effected on the 5th July. The opposition of the disloyal party at Basle, however, still continued, and Henry wrote again to Pope Eugenius. "If this continues," he says, "Christian princes should come together and with their united forces rally to the support of your Holiness and the Chair of Peter; leaving no means untried to secure pacific unity. Lest there should be any doubt whatever of the filial sincerity of our adherence to and our venera-

* *Beckynton Correspondence*, pp. 37, 53.

tion for Your Holiness and the Holy Roman Church, over which you so worthily preside, we think well to make known to Your Holiness that with all our vassals and subjects we will come to your assistance, and serve you, as hitherto we have always shown to Your Holiness and the Roman Church untainted and sincere obedience, reverence, and filial devotion." He adds that he will take every means to get other princes to do the same, and " secure obedience and unity with the Roman Church under Your Blessedness and Your Successors." *

The pious King Henry likewise wrote several letters at this time to the Emperor Frederick urging him again to strong action, and he sent the Bishop of Rochester and another prelate to emphasize the need of united action if the bark of Peter is to be brought safely out of the raging seas to a safe port.†

In 1439, on hearing that the Greeks were once more united with the Western Church, Henry wrote to Pope Eugenius IV expressing his fervent gratitude to God for this good

* *Beckynton Correspondence*, pp. 94-8.
† *Ibid.*, p. 93.

result.  He attributes the restoration of the
unity of the Church to the paternal patience,
vigilance, and care of the Holy Father.  " We
confess," he says, " that directly we had seen
Your letter announcing these good tidings,
we were filled with joy.  Oh! the wonderful
goodness of God!  Oh! His wondrous loving-
kindness! which has allowed us in our days
to witness the healing of the divisions of our
Mother Church His Spouse, caused so many
ages back by the sins of men, and which
during many generations seemed beyond all
remedy.  Oh! how many kings and princes
have desired to see what we now behold!"
Henry adds that he looks upon this as an
earnest of future blessings, and that he has
already given orders for public prayers and
processions in thanksgiving to God.*  When
a short time after this the news came that the
Armenians had also been reconciled to the
One Church, the King again wrote to the
Pope expressing his joy.  " The submission of
the Greeks," he says, " was indeed a blessed
work, and this bringing back of other sheep,
long wandering outside of the Church's fold,
crowns the work.  By the labour of your

* *Beckynton Correspondence*, p. 50.

Blessedness in this Holy Synod of Florence, the Easterns have been called to the Unity, Obedience, and Faith of the Roman Church." This event has also been celebrated by public prayers and processions of heartfelt thanks to God.*

* *Beckynton Correspondence*, p. 52.

## VII

## THE BOOK OF THE KING'S
## MIRACLES

IT has already been pointed out that a contemporary register of the miracles attributed to King Henry VI was kept at Windsor.
These records were written in English, and
Harpesfield, although he had not seen the
original volumes, speaks of having examined a
Latin translation made, as he supposed, in
view of the process of canonization of the
saintly King, which had been commenced by
the Roman authorities. It is fairly certain
that the Latin translation spoken of by Harpesfield is that which is now among the Royal
MSS. in the British Museum. As this
volume had belonged to Archbishop Cranmer,
many of whose books had formerly been in the
Canterbury archives, Harpesfield as Archdeacon of Canterbury, who had access to
other records of the See, would no doubt have
examined it there.

The translator, who desired to remain unknown, and whose name, even in his day, Harpesfield could not discover, as he tells us, was a monk. He calls himself " John," and it has been suggested with some probability that he was the John Blackman, originally secretary of the saintly Henry VI, the author of the intimate life already described, who subsequently became a monk in the Charter House at London. The volume, at present among the Royal MSS., is really the first draft, much corrected, of the proposed translation. These corrections, mainly of style, are numerous throughout the volume; and the 135 miracles therein recorded are selections from some 300 which, as the translator tells us, were to be found entered in the English volumes or registers kept at the tomb of the saintly King at Windsor. The monk " John " states that he had received the English records from John Morgan, the Dean of Windsor, who, with other Canons of the Collegiate Church, such as Oliver King, subsequently Bishop of Bath and Wells, kept a faithful record of the graces and blessings received at the tomb at Windsor. Dean Morgan's name appears many times in the records of these miracles

as having welcomed the pilgrims to Windsor,
when they came to return thanks for graces
obtained by their recourse to the King's intercession. He took from them their testimony
as to facts and dates and more than once
himself joined in their thanksgivings in the
Church. The Latin translator tells us that
the Windsor book of the miracles was sent to
him by the hands of a friend of Dean Morgan,
and the date of beginning the work of turning
the English into Latin and making the selection would have been some time before 1496,
when John Morgan was made Bishop of St.
David's. In the course of translating, the
monk records the change by speaking of
Morgan as formerly Dean, now Bishop, of
St. David's. It is useful here to note that
besides the testimony of these miracles actually
set down in this book, there is clear evidence
in these records of the devotion to the saintly
King which existed in all parts of England.
These wonders are worked in all parts of the
land. In Northumberland and Durham, in
Sussex and Wales, etc., they are certified as
having taken place at various times. It is
apparent, and there is no room for doubting,
that the English people very generally

spontaneously turned to the holy King Henry for help before the throne of God, in all manner of circumstances and difficulties and dangers. They evidently did this quite naturally, as if, indeed, there was a practically common belief in the efficacy of his intercession in heaven. The translator in his introduction likens the great extension of this popular devotion to the King, to a vine which sends its suckers out to take widespread roots; or to a palm tree planted by the running waters, which spreads its branches abroad on every side. "We have," he writes, "to admire rather than to explain this gracious goodness of God; the excellence of His power is proved more by His works than taught by any sermons." Now at Windsor everyone can see for himself the extraordinary reputation for sanctity and the wonderful power exercised by the holy man, Henry, late King of England. His life in this world was remarkable for humility, piety, patience, etc., and indeed for the exercise of all the virtues. His death also was precious in God's sight, as is shown by numberless great miracles. . . . Who does not recognize this in every part of England, and even in foreign lands ?  What church is there that does not admire and rejoice in proclaiming his greatness ? or what has not experienced the effect of one or other of these miracles ?  I am sure that this country will rejoice that such an abundance of supernatural grace has been showered upon us.  For indeed, if any reader will examine this record with care he will find evidence of really great miracles wrought by the Almighty God, the Worker of all miracles; not only for the renown of the great King, but for the glory of the whole Church.

These miracles were inscribed in the book which, as is asserted, was begun to be kept at Windsor within two years after the precious body was buried there.  The various accounts were written in English with the attestations to their truth, by the actors and their witnesses.  "They are here [*i.e.* in the translation] given: not indeed all the series, but such examples as I [the translator] believe to be most useful to the reader. I consider that all the cases here set forth are useful and afford clear evidence of the virtue of the saintly man; but they are not all of equal weight and importance.  For this reason," he continues, "after consultation it seemed best to me to take only those which manifest clearly the King's renown. The rest I do not intend to put altogether aside or reject, but to leave them for some other time."

The writer then turns for help in his work " to the sweet Father and Soldier of Christ, the most noble King Henry, the hope of so many and the consoler of those in trouble. Intercede to supply my deficiency with those authorities of the great Mother Church that they may recognize the common opinion of thy Sanctity. This belief is not founded on any silly popular superstition, but is proved by God's mercy and proclaimed publicly by the frequency of the miracles." The writer's hope and belief was, without prejudice to the ecclesiastical judgement, that the sanctity of the holy King would be recognized. In his prologue to the miracles the author again expresses his wish to carry out the task the Dean of Windsor had asked him to undertake. One reason for this desire is that he " may give pleasure to the great and indeed the enormous number of pilgrims to Windsor, who crowd along the public roads and lanes in the belief that they will receive more abundant grace

from God, the more these works of charity by
the holy King are known." *

The *Book of the King's Miracles* is composed,
besides prologues, etc., of four different collections of miracles; each preceded by an index
or table of contents. The first set of these
miracles contain twenty-eight, with a full and
minute description of what had happened and
how, together with the dates upon which the
events took place in the years 1481-1490.†
The second set gives particulars of sixty-seven
miracles, preceded also by an index. It is
stated in the prologue to this section, to which
reference has already been made, that they
are merely a selection from the 300 cases
registered in an English book left at Windsor,
to which a special number is affixed in each
case.‡ The third collection of these wonderful events includes twenty-four of these
miracles, and they belong to the period of the
first seven years of King Henry VII, that is
from 1485 to 1492.§ Finally, a fourth
set gives the particulars, circumstances, and
dates of sixteen miracles. An important

* B.M. Royal MS. 13, c. viii, fol. 33.
† *Ibid.*, fol. 6 *seqq.*
‡ *Ibid.*, fol. 33 *seqq.*      § *Ibid.*, fol. 86 *seqq.*

matter to note is the fact that the manuscript
clearly shows that it has been used to sift the
evidence given to prove the miracle. There
has evidently been a serious attempt to examine into the truth of the assertions made.
Thus, against some in a hand different from
that of the translator are to be found such ex-
pressions as *probatum* (proven), *non-probatum*
(not proven), *non referitur* (the witnesses or
parties not being forthcoming), etc. In one
or two cases we find a note to the effect " let
N. or M. be examined." Thus in the case of
a miracle said to have been wrought in
Sussex on 30th September 1495, in favour of
a priest named John Reynald, there is written
" let John Reynald, and John Key and John
Stranger be examined." Finally, there is
entered in the margin the note *probatum*
(proven).

There was obviously, as already stated,
great care taken at Windsor in taking the
original depositions of the miracles. In one
case, for example, a miracle supposed to have
been wrought at Sheppey in Kent on " the
tuesday after the Feast of Corpus Christi, was
sworn to by the witnesses on the tomb of the
holy King at Windsor." And, on the same

and according to the custom of children, she took leave to go out from her father's house, and so doing, wandered into a neighbouring garden. In this garden there was a fish pond, and somehow or other, she fell into the pond and was entirely submerged, with no one to help her. An hour later her parents returned, and not finding the child, enquired for her from their friends and neighbours. Not finding any trace of her, they were in great distress. Later the owner of the garden came by chance into it, and saw the body of the child entirely under the water and motionless in the middle of the pond. At his call a great number of people came running to assist him to bring the body out of the water to the bank. The child was apparently dead, and the parents and neighbours in their distress had recourse to prayer. All fell on their knees to the ground and raised their voices to heaven, begging the help of the Blessed Mother of God and of His most holy soldier King Henry, by whose prayers they hoped to have at least the grace of consolation. Then suddenly, before the eyes of all, the child began to come to herself and to move. After a short time, and after a great quantity of water had come out of the child's mouth, she suddenly exclaimed: 'O my God! and thou the most blessed King Henry, help me.' These exact circumstances were deposed to on oath by the forty witnesses on the King's tomb at Windsor." *

In one part of this volume the author speaks of the immense number of spiritual graces which were obtained by the intercession of the saintly King. Very generally the people turned to him in their difficulties and needs, but such things, says the author, by their very nature and frequency could not be registered. In another part of the book it is stated as a fact that the reputation for sanctity was daily increasing by reason of the many miracles and graces obtained by having recourse to the saintly King's protection. There were some people, of course, who questioned the truth of these wonders, and who even scoffed at them. One instance is recorded in these pages of a man who derided them, and declared his disbelief of all miracles in general. He was, however, converted to the truth by being himself cured of a painful disease through the intercession of the holy King. Half in

* B.M. Royal MS. 13, c. viii, fol. 68.

mockery he had said that he would himself vow to go on pilgrimage to the King's tomb if he were freed from his sufferings. God showed him this mercy through the intercession of King Henry, and he went as he had promised to Windsor to return thanks for his own cure and there made a declaration on oath of the circumstances, before M. H. Seymour, one of the canons of the royal collegiate establishment.

There are many very astonishing cures given in the volume; here it must suffice to give some few notes, taken almost at haphazard, from its pages. At a place called Reyton, in Rutlandshire, a small child, the son of a man named John Hargrave, about fifteen months old, fell into the fire. It happened that on the feast of St. Hugh both parents went to attend the vespers of the day in the parish church, leaving the infant alone in the house, not taking care to set a guard round the fire which was burning on the hearth. When alone, by some means the child fell backwards with his head in the burning embers. Unable to help himself the little John had all his hair and the skin of his head burned off; and when his parents returned the whole house was filled with the smell of the burning, which even attracted to the place a number of the neighbours. They went in search of the mother and she hastened back in company of one named John Sherman. The infant was apparently dead, or on the point of death when they took it from the fire. The whole of its scalp was burnt off, a great blister covered its face, and there were other terrible injuries besides. John Hargrave, the father, the god-parents of the child, who had come to the house, and all the crowd of neighbours at once fell on their knees to pray Almighty God to save the life of the child, invoking also the intercession of the holy King Henry before the throne of God, and vowing to go to his tomb in thanksgiving if their prayers were heard. In less than an hour's time the child began to show signs of life, and in a brief time, "about the feast of St. Gregory the Pope," a new scalp was formed and it had entirely recovered. The parents and friends thereupon, on 6th May, came to Windsor to fulfil their vow to the saint. They first had a Mass of thanksgiving said in the chapel, and then displayed to all the head of the infant to show how it had entirely recovered. There were present at the time a goodly number of people, and amongst them some of the canons and masters of the college and one bishop. Before these their testimony was given under oath; and they hung up near to the tomb a votive offering in wax representing the cranium of the child. " This," adds the writer, " can be seen there to this day."

In 1485 a woman who had been blind for five years was cured at the King's tomb. Her name was Joan Sawyer, or Walsh, and she came from Buckingham, and the reputation of the miracle was spread far and wide: another case of a cure effected at Windsor was that of a man from Northamptonshire. For two years he had lost the use of his limbs. He had been brought to the shrine on horseback, but had to be helped into the church by two strong men, not being able to stand on his legs. He remained before the tomb, bowed in prayer, for two days, most earnestly asking the saintly King's help. He manifested great confidence in the prayers of the saint, and he obtained what he desired, for " on Monday after the feast of St. Michael, suddenly his pains disappeared, strength returned to his legs, and he was able to leave the church without aid." *

* B.M. Royal MS. 13, c. viii, fol. 57.

PORTRAIT FROM EYE CHURCH

# VIII

## *CULTUS* AND POPULAR DEVOTION TO THE SAINTLY KING HENRY

ALMOST immediately after the death of King Henry there was manifested a popular belief in his sanctity and in the many miracles wrought at his tomb. It has already been pointed out that images of the King were set up in cathedrals like York and Ripon and in numerous parish churches throughout England. In his interesting article in the *Dublin Review* (January 1921) Mr. Leonard Smith has collected many instances of this form of public veneration. At Algood, in Lincolnshire, he writes, there was a bequest to King Henry's Light which, presumably, burned before an image of the King; at Gately and at Barton Turf, in Norfolk, this image stood upon the rood screen. Eye Church, in Suffolk, possessed a painted portrait of the King in a royal mantle, with a large sceptre in his right hand, his head nimbed, and a curved band behind the shoulders bearing the inscription: HEN. REX.* A pair of beads of dogeon (boxwood) and an image of King Henry formed the bequest of Sir Robert Aubery, priest of a chantry in Lincoln Cathedral, to one Master Thorp in 1535; and at Windsor, where the hat and spurs of the King were venerated as most efficacious relics, little signs or tokens were made to be carried home by pilgrims.† The dagger that killed Henry VI " schethe and all " was kept until the Reformation by the Augustinians at Caversham among other relics and offerings, such as " schroudes, candels, images of wax, crowches and brochys."‡ In the churchwardens' accounts of Pilton, Somerset, for 15 Hen. VII the valuables belonging to the church include

---

* See the *Journal of the British Archaeological Association* (Dec. 1880) for an account of this portrait, with a reproduction. Similar fifteenth-century paintings have been discovered in Warfield Church, Berkshire, and on the west wall of the nave of Wilton Church, Norfolk.

† See *Journal of the Brit. Arch. Assoc.* (Oct. 1845 and Sept. 1868) for some account of these, with plates.

‡ Wright, *Letters relating to the Suppression of the Monasteries* (Camden Soc.), p. 224.

" brochys of King Henry and one lytyle broche," badges or tokens most probably brought by pilgrims from Windsor; and in the clerestory of Fairford Church, in Gloucestershire, his image was sculptured with those of Henry VII and of the Emperor-Saint, Henry of Germany.

To the above instances of images and paintings of Henry VI for devotional use in churches may be added: a sixteenth-century painting on glass in a window of Provost Hacombleyn's chantry in King's College, Cambridge; a wall painting, *temp*. Henry VII, in Alton Church, Hampshire. This last is nimbed, wears a red robe and ermine mantle and holds a sceptre.* Ancient representations of the King are also to be seen in the antechapel of All Souls College, Oxford; in St. Mary's Hall, Coventry, and in the church of Ashton-under-Lyne.† Lastly, on the screen at Ludham, in Norfolk, there is a painting of Henry VI, together with King Edmund the Martyr and Edward the Confessor.‡ Nor must there be forgotten the image on Prince

* Vide *Times* (21 December 1921).
† *Ibid.* (9 December 1921).
‡ *Ibid.* (3 December 1921).

Arthur's chantry in Worcester Cathedral and those on the lectern at King's College, Cambridge, and at Eton. A copy of the last-named in gold was the present made by the students at Eton to the Princess Mary on her marriage.

As an evidence of popular *cultus* of King Henry, even more striking than these images and paintings set up in the English churches, are the hymns, prayers, and short offices of the saintly King, which were evidently very numerous and many of which are still preserved. Some instances may here be given, without any attempt to arrange them in order of date or importance. An ancient " Bede roll " is preserved among the Trevelyan family papers, which contain several prayers and hymns to the saintly monarch. This part is headed: " Here ys a devoute prayer of Kyng Harre."* The first hymn begins:

> Gaude princeps populorum
> Dux et decus Britanorum
> Rex Henricus nomine.

and has some twelve verses recording the numerous virtues of the holy man. This is followed by the versicle: " Pray for us,

* *Trevelyan Papers* (Camden Soc.), i, 53.

HENRY VI

From a print after the painting on glass at King's College,
Cambridge

blessed Henry," etc., and the prayer in Latin:
" O Omnipotent and merciful God, who haſt
in numerous ways rendered the blessed Henry
King and Martyr illuſtrious by Thy glorious
miracles, and haſt mercifully at his saving
petition given health to the sick. Grant, we
beseech Thee, that when we honour him by
our prayers we may be assiſted by his help in
every temptation, difficulty, and adversity,
and progress by the example of his life. *Per
Deum*, etc."  This is followed on the same
Roll by another hymn under the title " another
prayer of Kynge Harre."  The saintly servant
of God is invoked as " Chriſti servus et
amicus, clarens jam miraculis "; as " Vir
magnae sanctitatis; vivit regno claritatis in
coelorum patria," and his many miracles are
extolled: "Visum reddet excaecatis, claudis
gressum et curvatis; lasis fert auxilium;
aegros sancit et languores; febres fugat gravi-
ores; procul in exilium."  Then the hymn
continues in praise of his virtuous life:

> Hic in vita multa passus,
> Caritate nunquam lassus
>   Inimicos diligit.
> Ejus pietas et benigna
> Mira mundo dedit signa
>   Quod sic pati voluit.

Miles Dei virtuosus
Cunctis fuit graciosus
    Malis bonum reddidit.
Gaudet nunc gens Anglicorum
De patrono quod eorum
    Deus Sanctus reddidit
O Rex (sancte) Anglicorum
Gubernatorque Francorum
    Te mox invocantibus
Esto tutum adjuvamen
Et fer semper relevamen
    Nobis deprecantibus.

℣. Ora pro nobis beate serve Dei Henrice.
℟. Ut digni, etc.

*Oratio.*

O God, the crown of Kings and Glory of Saints,
Grant that we may obtain, through the patronage of Thy
blessed servant Henry, that by Thy Grace rejoicing in
his memory, we may partake of the glory and crown of
life promised to those who love Thee, through Christ
our Lord. (*Translation.*)

From a fifteenth century MS. belonging
to the Pudsey family and preserved in the
Trevelyan papers,* there has come down to us
another salutation and prayer to King Henry:

Oratio beate Henrici Sexti Regis Angliae et Franciae.
Hic vir dispiciens mundum, et terrena triumphans
    divitias coelo condidit corde ore et manu
Ora pro nobis beate Henrice
    Ut digni, etc.

-------

* *Ut sup.* (Camden Soc.), i, 57, 58.

Deus qui unigenitum filium tuum, Dominum nostrum
Jesum Christum, famulo tuo Regi nostro Henrico
corpore et anima glorificatum demonstrare voluisti,
praesta quaesimus, ut eius meritis et precibus ad
aeternam fidem Domini nostri Jesu Christi et
visionem pertingere mereamur

Per Dominum nostrum, etc.

In the same collection of papers * there is the
following English prayer to the saintly King
written, as it would seem, for a pilgrimage to
the tomb at Windsor:

> As far as hope will yn length
> On the Kyng Henry I fix my mynde
> That by thy prayers I may have strenkith
> In vertuous lyfe my works to bynde
> Though I to thee have been unkynde
> Of wilfulness long tyme and space
> Of forgevness I aske the grace
> Hope hathe me movyde to seke this place
> In trust of socor by thyn old properte
> Was never man came beforne thi face
> Rebellion or oder yn adverite
> Off thyn compassion comaunded then go free
> Now for thi pety to hym that all shall deme
> Pray for me thy servant and pilgreme.

At the beginning of the *Book of the Miracles*

* *Ut sup.* (Camden Soc.), i, 59.

there is to be found * a hymn and prayer entitled:

*Salutatio gloriosi Militis Xpi. Henrici Regis Angliae Sexti cum oracuncula eidem.*

### The hymn begins:

Salve miles preciose, Rex Henrice generose palma vitis
    celice
In radice caritatis. Vernans flores sanctitatis viteque
    Angelice.

### And the last of the five verses is:

Salve quem rex seculorum, choris pingens Angelorum
Civem fecit patria fruentis
Te laudare cupientes. Tecum vita gloria
                    Amen.

*N.* Veniant ad te qui detrahebant tibi
    Et adorant vestigia pedum tuorum.

*Prayer.*

O loving Lord Jesus Christ, Salvation and Saviour of all who believe in Thee, Who willed that Thy beloved servant King Henry should be afflicted by the weight of many tribulations, in order that by the merits of his patience and most innocent life, by which Thy copious love may be displayed to the people by the glory of miracles, Grant we beseech Thee, that all, who rejoice in his glory and for Thee, or rather glorifying him in Thee, may praise his merits and be found worthy of share in the company of his beatitude and both here and in the future obtain this by his merits. (*Translation.*)

---

* B.M. Royal MS. 13, c. vii, fol. iv.

Again, on the fly-leaf of an early primer preserved at Ushaw College, Durham, is written:

O blyssed King so full of vertue
The flowr of all Knighthood that never was syled
Thou pray for us to Christe Jhesu
And to hys mother Mary myld
In all thy workys thou was never wyld
But full of grace and charitie
Mercifull ever to man and chylde
Now sweyt Kynge Harre, pray for me.

Among the Harleian MSS. in the British Museum (MS. 2887) is the following:

ORATIO BEATI HENRICI REX [*sic*] ANGLIE.

Domine Ihu Xpe qui me creasti, redemisti et predestinasti ad hoc quod sum, Tu scis quid de me facere vis, fac de me secundum voluntatem tuam cum misericordia.

This prayer is printed in the Horae of 1510 (Wynkyn de Worde) and the date is supposed to be 1504.* In the same MS. are these other prayers:

ALIA ORO.

Dne Ihu Xpe qui solus habes sapientiam, Tu scis que mihi peccatori expediunt prout Tibi placet et sicut in oculis majestatis tue videtur de me peccatore ita fiat cum misericordia ; Qui cum, etc. Amen.

Pater Nr.                              Ave Maria.

De Beato Henrico

---

* *Vide* Hearne, *Otterbourne*, i, Pref., p. liv.

*Oratio.*

Rex Henricus pauperum et ecclesiae defensor, ad
misericordiam pronus, in caritate fervidus, clerum decoravit quem Deus sic beatificavit.

℣. Ora pro nobis devote Rex Henrice.
℟. Ut digni efficiamur promissionibus Xpi.

*Oremus.*

Deus sub cujus ineffabili providencia universi Reges
regnant et imperant qui devotissimum Henricum Anglorum Regem caritate fervidum miseris et afflictis
semper compassum omni bonitate clemenciaq: conspicuum ut pie creditur inter angelos conumerare dignatus es: concede propitius ut eo cum omnibus sanctis
intervenientibus hostium nostrorum superbia conteratur
moribus et quod malum est procul pellatur palma donetur et gratia Sancti Spiritus nobis misericordiam poscentibus ubiq: adesse dignetur.  Qui vivis in gloria regnas
cum potencia moderans saecula cuncta.  Amen.

Mr. H. H. E. Craster, sub-librarian of the
Bodleian, Oxford, has kindly sent me the
following devotional prayers from a MS. of
Sarum Hours in University College, Oxford
(MS. 8, fol. 87).

*Oratio bona ad beatum Henricum regem.*
O bone rex regum Nos protege ab hoste maligno
Henrici meritis Vitam sine fine vivendo
Cum rectis animis Letemur in ethere summo
Et terre fundator Hominum deus atque redemptor

Suscipe pro merito Henrici martiris almi
Qui pro salute Gens anglica munera laudis.

*Versiculus.* Alme Dei martir Henrice, tu memoriam
agentibus auxiliare.

*Oratio.*

*Oremus.* Deus cuius posse maximum, scire verissimum,
et peroptimum velle in splendoribus sanctorum relucet;
presta quesumus, ut qui nostrorum actuum leuitate grauiter
premimur, tui vigoris brachio, splendoris radio, amoris
pondere, subleuemur.

The existence of a commemoration of the
saintly King in so many manuscripts and
printed *Horae* is a proof of the widespread
devotion of the English people to him. His
name, it is true, is not found entered in the
Calendars of Saints, nor in the Missals of the
period. This is what would be expected, since
his canonization had not been decreed by the
Church, and in no wise militates against the
popular *cultus* of the servant of God.

William Maskell, in his *Monumenta Litu-
alia** prints an officium " de beato rege
Henrico."

*Ant.* Rex Henricus sis amicus, etc.

*V.* Ora pro nobis devote rex Henricus.

*R.* Ut per te, etc.

*Oratio.*

Praesta quaesimus Omnipotens et Misericors dominus
ut qui devotissimi Regis Henrici, etc.

---

* Ed. 1882, iii, 369.

K

He then prints:

Hanc orationem summus Pontifex Sixtus Romae quartus composuit ad laudem et honorem gloriosissimi regis Henrici regis Angliae post conquest sexti.

Beatus rex Henricus pauperum, etc.

℣. Ora pro nobis beate Henrice pauperum et ecclesiae, etc.

### Oremus.

Deus qui beatum regem Henricum tuum sanctum militem, etc.

This is printed from a MS.* in the British Museum.

This Sixtine devotion does not appear in any Sarum Horae, but in substance it is found in the York Horae printed by Nic. le Roux at Rouen, 1536.   Here it runs:

#### COMMEMORATIO DE SANCTO HENRICO.

Rex Henricus pauperum et ecclesiae defensor, ad misericordiam semper pronus, in Charitate fervidus, pietate deditus clerum decoravit, quem Deus magnis virtutibus et miraculis mirabiliter in populo suo Anglorum beatificavit.

℣. Ora pro nobis princeps Henrice.

℟. Ut digni efficiamur promissionibus Christi.

### Oratio.

Deus sub cujus ineffabile providentia universi reges regnant et inperant, qui devotissimum regem Henricum

---

* Harl. MS. 5793.

Anglorum regem, in charitate fervidum, miseris
afflictis et male habentibus semper compassum, omni
bonitate innocentiaque conspicuum ut pie creditur inter
Angelos collocare dignatus es, concede propicius, ut
ipso cum omnibus sanctis intervenientibus hostium nostrorum tollatur superbia, morbus et omne quod malum
est a nobis procul pellatur, palma donetur et gratia
Sancti Spiritus nobis misericordiam tuam poscentibus
semper adesse dignetur.

Qui vivis, etc.

These and similar devotions and prayers
to King Henry are found very generally. For
example, in the larger and fuller 4to Horae
of Wynkyn de Worde, 1502 and 1523;
Bryckman, 1516; Ruremund, 1520 and
1531; Pynson, 1522. It is said also that
these prayers were printed in various editions
of Regnault, the most prolific printer of
Sarum books.

An *Oratio de Beato Rege Henrico* also appears
in Caxton's *XV Oes* in 1491; and in Wynkyn
de Worde's Horae, or *XV Oes*, of 1491
(printed at the commaundement of Elisa-
beth and pryncesse Margarite) on vellum.
Here it is entitled " Oratio de Beato Rege
Henrico, a prayer to holy King Henry."
Canon Hoskins, in his *Catalogue of Primers
and Books of Hours*, notes copies of this as

existing at Lambeth, Bodley, and two copies in the Cambridge University Library.*

The above noted instances of the devotions, prayers, hymns, and commemorations in honour of the saintly King Henry will be more than sufficient to show that his *cultus* was widely spread throughout England up to the very eve of the Reformation.

The *Acta Sanctorum* † says that the *obitus* of King Henry was entered in red letters in the Calendar of a Sarum Breviary printed in 1557. The old *English Martyrology* of Wilson, in great use by the Catholics in the days of persecution, has his name entered sub *Nomine Sancti Regis Henrici*. The constant tradition of Catholics in regard to the sanctity of this holy English King may best be summed up in the words of the authoritative Menology published by the authority of the English hierarchy in 1887:

### Henry VI King a.d. 1471

" The calamities of a long reign on earth were the means by which God was pleased to prepare this saintly Prince for the inheritance

* Most of this information I owe to the kind interest of my friend, Mr. Falkner.

† Maii v, p. 127.

of a Kingdom of endless bliss in the future world. The life of Henry was blameless from the first dawn of reason to its close. His enemies were many but none of them could deny his purity, his devotion, his patience under trials, or his placable disposition. He did what his unhappy circumstances allowed for the benefit of his people; he oppressed them with no burdensome taxes or extraordinary imposts, but wished all to live in peace and contentment, as well the meanest of his subjects as the great nobles. He had always the interests of religion most at heart, and founded the Colleges of Eton and King's at Cambridge.

" After his cruel murder, the good King was buried at Chertsey Abbey, and it was not long before miracles began to attest his sanctity. These, in the course of time, became so numerous that Richard III was induced to translate his remains to St. George's Chapel at Windsor; perhaps as an act of reparation for his share in the great crime. From that time the sick and afflicted from all parts of the country had recourse to the intercession of Henry, and long lists of well-authenticated graces were drawn up. Henry VII made great efforts to obtain his canonization, and it appears that Pope Julius II was prepared to grant the petition, when the death of the King postponed the proceedings, which were never resumed. The sentiment of the nation, however, has ever regarded King Henry VI of Windsor as a saint, and compilers of our more recent martyrologies have given him a place among the eminent servants of God."

# INDEX

LONDON : CHARLES WHITTINGHAM AND GRIGGS (PRINTERS), LTD.
CHISWICK PRESS, TOOKS COURT, CHANCERY LANE.